Teaching Reading through the Arts

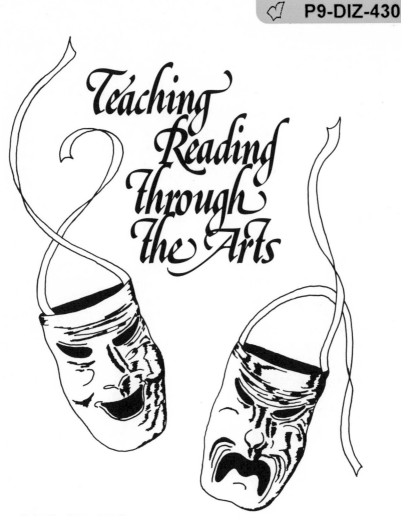

John E. Cowen, Editor
Teaneck, New Jersey, Public Schools

For the Reading through the Arts Committee
With an Introduction by M. Jerry Weiss

ira

INTERNATIONAL READING ASSOCIATION
800 Barksdale Road   Newark, Delaware 19711

INTERNATIONAL READING ASSOCIATION

Copyright 1983 by the
International Reading Association, Inc.

Library of Congress Cataloging in Publication Data
Main entry under title:

Teaching reading through the arts.

Bibliography: p.
1. Reading. 2. Language arts. 3. Arts—Study
and teaching. 4. Arts and children. I. Cowen,
John E. II. International Reading Association.
Reading and the Arts Committee.
LB1050.T37   1983   372.4′1   82-12755
ISBN 0-87207-733-0

Contents

Foreword

Through art in its many forms humans seek to express their most important thoughts and values. Different individuals understand these ideas better through one art form than through another. To one person, music speaks with the greatest clarity; to another, it is a painting that conveys the most effective message; to still another, literature has the most immediate appeal. Regardless of the differences and preferences among those who experience art, the same basic messages are involved.

Because this is true, it is clear that appreciation of one art form can reinforce appreciation of another. If children experience the arts and relate their experience to their reading, both experiences are enhanced. Children can dance a poem as well as read it.

It is good when a group of creative teachers try to help other teachers with ideas for bringing the arts together and connecting them all with reading. It is not easy to do this when so much depends on the personality of the individual teacher. There are no firm "rules of the game." This volume presents some general principles and some specific procedures which have worked for *some* teachers with *some* children and may work for you.

OLIVE S. NILES

Preface

Teaching Reading through the Arts explores ways of using the arts—drama, television, music, art, and creative writing—as a major force in humanizing reading instruction and in the development of lifetime readers.

The integration of the arts with reading offers many creative approaches to reading and classroom teachers to provide their students with educational experiences that will not only help them master basic skills but will also affect their capacity for aesthetic appreciation, growth, and sensitivity.

The "back-to-basics" movement in education has caused some concerned educators to fear that the arts will eventually be stripped from the curriculum, and has given rise to a counter-movement to guard against such an eventuality. This fear was somewhat relieved in the spring of 1979 when the Council for Basic Education announced that the arts "should be part of everyone's basic education."

This IRA publication attempts to offer rationale and insights as well as practical suggestions for the effective use of the arts in the reading curriculum.

JEC

Introduction

Teaching Reading through the Arts is a personal realization that students use a variety of techniques—art, music, drama, film, dance, writing—to indicate what impact reading has made upon their lives. In an era of accountability, it is extremely important to recognize that a creative teacher can instill a sensitivity to the worlds of print within students in many content areas. The arts are not frivolous experiences. They are the expressions of souls reacting to ideas in a complex, multi-splendored world. A song, a play, or a puppet show is a reading activity! Mastery of many reading skills can be effectively demonstrated through a student's use of an art form to reveal what learning is taking place. Facts and opportunities or personal interpretations are the substances of a love of reading and an appreciation of learning.

Parents, teachers, and administrators should remember that students are human beings, and not behavioral robots who respond with computerized results and statistical scores to management systems and drill-skill activities. These activities are narrow and constraining in the development of literate students.

Albert Einstein stated in *The New York Times*, October 5, 1952:

> It is not enough to teach man a specialty. Through it he may become a kind of useful machine but not a harmoniously developed personality. It is essential that the student acquire an understanding of and a lively feeling for values. He must acquire a vivid sense of the beautiful and of the morally good. Otherwise, he—with his specialized knowledge—more closely resembles a well-trained dog than a harmoniously developed person. He must learn to understand the motives of human beings, their illusions, and their sufferings in order to acquire a proper relationship to individual fellow-men and to the community.
>
> These precious things are conveyed to the younger generation through personal contact with those who teach, not—or at least not in the main—through textbooks. It is this that primarily constitutes and preserves culture. This is what I have in mind when I recommend the "humanities" as important, not just dry specialized knowledge in the fields of history and philosophy.

Overemphasis on the competitive system and premature specialization on the ground of immediate usefulness kill the spirit on which all cultural life depends, specialized knowledge included.

It is also vital to a valuable education that independent critical thinking can be developed in the young human being, a development that is greatly jeopardized by overburdening him with too much and with too varied subjects [point system]. Overburdening necessarily leads to superficiality. Teaching should be such that what is offered is perceived as a valuable gift and not as a hard duty.

Certainly, Einstein's remarks deserve serious thought about the humanizing forces needed in education. This volume is an attempt to share ideas about the effective use of the arts in conjunction with a reading program. All of the authors are writing from their experiences. The emphasis in this monograph is on the practical. Tomorrow's talented performers on stage and/or screen, on canvas, and in print, may owe their enthusiasm to those dedicated teachers who have helped them see that the literature of the world is, indeed, a most valuable source of ideas worthy of new creative expression.

M. Jerry Weiss
Jersey City State College

Reading, Television, and Theater Arts

Reading and Film, the Liveliest Art

Carole A. Cox
Louisiana State University

Film, the liveliest art, can enrich, expand, and enliven the teaching of reading. The art of the film and the act of reading are both communication skills, and may be linked in the classroom through many concrete activities related to motivation for reading, vocabulary expansion, reading as a thinking process, critical reading, extending reading, and creative reading. The power of film to make us feel can also make it a powerful tool in the hands of any teacher who wishes to use the arts to humanize reading instruction.

Since success in learning to read is in large part dependent on the child's language life, film study is a natural asset to the reading program. Creative filmmakers have produced many children's films which can provide exciting stimuli for dynamic oral discussions, which in turn create a healthy climate for thinking and reacting to an art form as a basis for verbal interaction between children, vocabulary growth, and other reading-related activities.

As a suggested beginning filmography for film study for intermediate and upper-grade children, a recent children's film poll (Cox, 1975) produced the following top ten children's films out of a choice of twenty-four:

A Top Ten of Children's Films

1. *The Case of the Elevator Duck* (Learning Corporation of America, 1974)
2. *The Fur Coat Club* (Learning Corporation of America, 1973)

3. *The Blue Dashiki: Jeffrey and His Neighbors* (Encyclopedia Britannica, 1969)
4. *Clown* (Learning Corporation of America, 1969)
5. *Catch the Joy* (Pyramid, 1970)
6. *The Cow* (Churchill, 1970)
7. *The Daisy* (Macmillan, 1967)
8. *Rock in the Road* (Macmillan, 1968)
9. *Hansel and Gretel* (Encyclopedia Britannica, 1973)
10. *Hopscotch* (Churchill, 1972)

Films like these can be used by teachers to motivate open-minded discussions which draw on the child's own feelings and responses to the art of the film. Many teachers using film in the classroom, however, may be uneasy about what to do when the lights go on after a film has been shown. Long conditioned by verbal discipline, they may attempt to force generalizations out of a film discussion even though this may not be the best way to deal with film art—a visual and kinetic medium which is perhaps more elusive than literature.

One film study technique which has successfully met this challenge is called the Image-Sound Skim, developed by film educator Richard Lacey (Lacey, 1972). Here is how it works: Students view the film and then share their feelings and communicate their ideas without fear of being wrong. The main purpose of the Image-Sound Skim is to allow the children to reorchestrate the movie by prompting each other's memory of the images and sounds of the film, learning how others perceive, and gathering enough concrete information about the film to gain insights for deeper exploration.

An illustration of this type of discussion (the level of sensibility and the perceptions on which verbalizations are based) is this fourth grade Image-Sound Skim stimulated by a viewing of the film *Rainshower* (Churchill, 1967), an impressionistic study of the birth, life, and death of a summer storm:

- I felt wet; I felt like wiping my face.
- I liked the way the film showed clouds reflected in a window. (This led to a discussion of the ways the filmmaker used the reflection technique in ponds and puddles.)
- I saw the day get darker and lighter because of clouds moving, but I didn't actually see the clouds—just the shadows.
- I saw each raindrop on the leaves.
- It was different from films you usually see in school; more interesting; less talking; it didn't need talking; I liked it better.
- You don't always need words to express your ideas; you can use pictures and sound, too, and it might even show your ideas better.

- The water made rhythm like music.
- The music fit the pictures and their feelings.
- The film could have ended differently. (Several children made suggestions and analogies with other films that end in different ways to achieve a certain feeling, and mentioned that some movies leave you with a question at the end.)

Reading-related activities which may follow film Image-Sound Skims are myriad. Film-related sight vocabulary may be introduced during or after these discussions and these high-interest words may be the basis for further word analysis. Reviews of films seen in class, on television, or commercial films, may be written by children for others to read and share through a card file, film review newspaper, or reviews posted on a bulletin board. Further analysis of films may be developed by producing flip books of films. These are small (approximately 2 x 4 inches), thick, stapled, blank books. Children may draw in one bit of action from a film on each page, in sequence, so that when the pages of the book are flipped, a moving impression of the film is seen. Children may also respond to film viewing by producing a shooting script, or storyboard of the film. Storyboards are sheets with four large squares to frame scenes in a vertical column of the left-hand side. The right-hand side of the page allows for comments, dialogue, shooting directions, and sound effects. It is necessary for children to make good use of the skills of sequencing and ordering when producing a storyboard, in order to communicate to others their feelings about a film.

Bookmaking is another film-related reading activity. Why not reverse the usual process of making films from books and encourage children to create books from films they have seen, or merge ideas from films and children's literature with their own experiences to create new impressions? Several critical reading skills come into play here. In order to effectively communicate a film's plot, narrative, characterizations, settings, images and moods, children must be able to outline, order, and sequence the film; interrelate visuals, symbols, and words; identify with story characters; perceive relationships; use imagination; and form sensory impressions and encode these impressions in pictures and words to communicate with others through the reading process.

An awareness of the strong bond that can tie film art and literature together can also be developed if children are introduced to certain filmmakers, picture book illustrators, and children's authors who have recognized and exploited this bond through their own artistic creations. Gerald McDermott is a filmmaker-turned-bookmaker who has transformed all of his famous short animated films (such as *The Stonecutter, The Magic Tree*, and *Anansi the Spider*) into picture book form. *Arrow to the Sun*, created simultaneously as a film and a book, won the Caldecott Award for 1975. With McDermott's work as a model, children can see and appreciate the tight knit which can exist between film art and the art of book creation, and can be motivated to create their own books from films.

Other famous author/illustrators can provide models for children. Chorao's *Ida Makes a Movie*, for example, explores the melodramatic events of a precocious personified cat, Ida, who creates her own Super 8 film, and wins all the prizes at a California film festival. A simple follow up to a reading of this book and, perhaps, a prelude to actual Super 8 filmmaking in the classroom could be the making of a film without a camera, using the draw-on technique. This requires either clear 16mm film leader, or a discarded 16mm film which has been cleaned of film emulsion with a solution of water and bleach. Children may then draw on the film with good quality marking pens and colored India ink designed for acetate. When the film is projected, their abstract images, colorful designs, simple figures, or words show on the screen as a fascinating display of light, color, and movement. This filmmaking activity can help children appreciate and understand the plastic nature of the film medium in addition to allowing them a great deal of creative expression through an existing, visual, tactile, and kinetic art form.

Film is art; film is language; film is fun. The relevancy of film can put reading into focus for today's media-oriented student. Film study, filmmaking, and film-related literature can facilitate a child's ability to use words freely and spontaneously in the communication process. It is this vital, dynamic, and moving quality of film that makes it a natural double feature with reading in the elementary classroom.

Film-Related Children's Books

Chorao, K. *Ida makes a movie.* New York: Seabury, 1975. Ida is a personified cat who makes a Super 8 film with the children in her neighborhood and wins the grand prize at a California film festival.

Lobel, A. *Martha the movie mouse.* New York: Harper & Row, 1966. Martha is a lonely little mouse who befriends a lonely movie projectionist, becomes a film fan, and ends up starring on the stage of the movie theatre before each show.

McDermott, G. *Anansi, the spider.* Holt, 1972 (Caldecott Honor Book).

McDermott, G. *Arrow to the sun.* Viking, 1974 (Caldecott Medal).

McDermott, G. *The magic tree.* Holt, 1973.

McDermott, G. *The stonecutter.* Viking, 1975. All of McDermott's picture books exist as original films as well. *Anansi, the spider* and *The magic tree* are adaptations of African folktales; *Arrow to the sun* is an adaptation of a native American legend; and *The stonecutter* is the retelling of a Japanese folktale.

Sendak, M. *In the night kitchen.* Harper & Row, 1970. Movie imagery in this picture book fantasy include scenes reminiscent of a 1930s musical set and sound stage and three cooks who are obviously a tribute to Oliver Hardy.

Cox

Adult References

Cox, C. *Film preference patterns of fourth and fifth grade children.* Unpublished dissertation, University of Minnesota, 1975.

Lacey, R. *Seeing with feeling, film in the classroom.* Philadelphia: W.B. Saunders, 1972.

Readers Theatre in the Classroom

Mary Stuart Taylor
La Mesa-Spring Valley School District, California

Readers Theatre is an oral interpretation of scripts developed from many kinds of literature, such as novels, short stories, poems, essays, and folktales. It differs from other forms of dramatic presentations in that scripts are usually carried and read or glanced at, even though performers may have memorized their lines. No costumes, props, or special lighting effects are required. It can be rehearsed and performed in the classroom.

The chief purpose of Readers Theatre is "to increase the understanding and appreciation of literature on the parts of those who participate through performing or through witnessing the performance" (Post, 1979). It features the student's personal involvement with literature. "It is one of the very best ways to introduce young people to the world's wealth of literary materials" (Coger & White, 1967).

Readers Theatre is a creative approach to motivate students from all grades to read and enjoy themselves in the reading process. Through Readers Theatre techniques, reading becomes a performing art. It may be used successfully with children who are experiencing reading difficulties as well as with those of average and superior reading abilities.

For your first production, begin with a short story or script (one or two pages) that you like. Your enthusiasm is important to the success of the project. Read the story to the class with dramatic flair, in order to ascertain whether a group of children would be interested in being performers. Following the initial reading, select those children who volunteer to perform and give them a copy of the script.

The simplest way to adapt a short story to script form for group reading is to eliminate the "he said" and "she saids" unless they seem appropriate for the mood and clarity of the story. *Why the Elephant Never Forgets* was written as a script for Readers Theatre by Joan Chase Bowden, San Diego author of children's books. A portion of it is presented here in narrative form to illustrate how to create a script from a short story.

Once upon a time there was a rhinoceros who had a terrible memory. "Now let's see," pondered the rhinoceros. "What's my name? Alice? Albert? Agnes? Alvin?"

His memory was so bad that he couldn't remember his numbers. He couldn't add. "One plus one equals three," said the rhinoceros, looking puzzled. He couldn't subtract or multiply. The rhinoceros scratched his head and said, "One minus one equals twenty-four. One times one equals six hundred and seventy-five."

He couldn't even remember what went on a sesame seed bun. He said, "Two all-beef fatties, special moss, lettuce, fleas, tickles, bunions. . . ."

His friends liked him. One friend turned to another saying enthusiastically, "I like him! Do you like him?" The other friend answered, "He's a dum-dum. But he's cute."

But the rhinoceros was very unhappy. He cried and cried. Then one day his Fairy Godmother came and said, "Hello. I am your Fairy Godmother. What is your wish?"

The original script reads as follows:

Why the Elephant Never Forgets
by Joan Chase Bowden

Characters	Narrator 1	Friend 2
	Narrator 2	Fairy Godmother
	Rhinoceros	Elephant
	Friend 1	

Narrator 1	Once upon a time there was a rhinoceros who had a terrible memory.
Rhinoceros	Now, let's see. What's my name? Alice? Albert? Agnes? Alvin?

Narrator 2	His memory was so bad that he couldn't remember his numbers. He couldn't add.
Rhinoceros	(looking puzzled) One plus one equals three.
Narrator 1	He couldn't subtract or multiply.
Rhinoceros	(scratching his head) One minus one equals twenty-four. One times one equals six hundred and seventy-five.
Narrator 2	He couldn't even remember what went on a sesame seed bun.
Rhinoceros	Two all-beef fatties, special moss, lettuce, fleas, tickles, bunions....
Narrator 1	His friends liked him.
Friend 1	I like him! Do you like him?
Friend 2	He's a dum-dum. But he's cute.
Narrator 2	But the rhinoceros was very unhappy.
Rhinoceros	Boo hoo. Sob sob. Weep weep.
Narrator 1	Then one day his Fairy Godmother came and said:
Fairy Godmother	Hello. I am your Fairy Godmother. What is your wish?

After you have read the story and chosen the cast, the next step is to have the first reading with children taking turns reading the parts. At this point, no characters are assigned permanently to the students. The reason for this is to have flexibility in making the final selections. If one character's lines are more difficult to read than others, it is wise to match the reading ability of the student with the part.

After several meetings in which the group reads the script, you and the children together decide on a part for each child. The children are encouraged to take their scripts home to practice. Frequently, parents will help by reading the lines of the other characters.

The next step in developing a Readers Theatre activity is staging the performance. Narrators usually stand, placing their script on a music stand, while the rest of the cast is seated on classroom chairs. The floor plan for *Why the Elephant Never Forgets* appears in this manner:

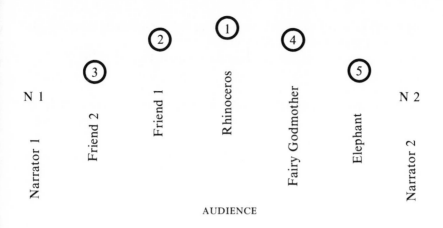

N 1   N 2

Narrator 1   Friend 2   Friend 1   Rhinoceros   Fairy Godmother   Elephant   Narrator 2

AUDIENCE

The final practices are devoted to refining good oral reading with expression and projection of voice, as well as adding appropriate movements and gestures to enhance the literature. Then the students should be ready to invite other classes to their performance.

Readers Theatre may be an informal classroom activity requiring fewer rehearsals in which groups of students perform for other members of their own class. It may also be a more formal presentation for an open house or a PTA meeting. For such occasions you may wish to use simple costumes, makeup, and props. In either case, it motivates students to read, teaches comprehension and listening skills, enriches literary appreciation, improves oral fluency, and develops a positive self-concept.

Some suggestions for material which lends itself to Readers Theatre are *Bremen Town Musicians; Chicken Little; The Three Billy Goats Gruff; The Three Little Pigs; Cinderella; Sleeping Beauty;* Dr. Suess' *The Sneetches, How the Grinch Stole Christmas, Horton Hears a Who, The Big Brag,* and *Thidwick, The Big-Hearted Moose*; also, *The Three Swine of Most Small Stature* by Lewy Olfson; Bernice Myers' *Shhhhh, It's a Secret*; Robert Kraus' *Leo the Late Bloomer*; Maurice Sendak's *Where the Wild Things Are*; E.B. White's *Charlotte's Web*; *Tikki Tikki Tembo* retold by Arlene Mosel; *The Cat Ate My Gymsuit* by Paula Danziger; *Ladies First* by Shel Silverstein; and *The Elephant Who Challenged the World* by James Thurber.

Poetry also may be adapted for Readers Theatre. "The Duel" by Eugene Field, "Disobedience" by A.A. Milne, and "The Day that Was that Day," by Amy Lowell are just a few examples.

You may wish to consider guiding your students in writing original scripts and also in helping them to adapt scripts from their favorite literature.

Readers Theatre offers a wealth of worthwhile language arts activities for the classroom. It can be a rewarding teaching experience and one that is fun for you and your students.

References

Coger, L.I., & White, M. *Readers theatre handbook: A dramatic approach to literature.* Glenview, Illinois: Scott, Foresman, 1967.
Post, R.M. Children's readers theatre. *Language Arts*, 1979, *56*, 262-267.

Television Viewing Skills

Milton Ploghoft
Ohio University
William D. Sheldon
Syracuse University

Introduction

The age of media is here, and arguments persist as to whether television hinders reading development. Television specials based on such literary works as *Roots, Shogun, The Summer of My German Soldier*, and *The Diary of Anne Frank* have stimulated interest in reading the original books. Book sales of these titles have zoomed. Research indicates that students will often choose books which have been introduced to them through films or television.

Certainly, reading specialists need to prepare students to deal with the impact of television on society. Television as an art form is also a strong tool for propaganda. Social and political issues can be presented quite effectively through documentary and dramatic presentations. History can be viewed almost nightly in every home in America. Students as well as adults are influenced by the ideas presented.

The authors of this chapter worked as consultants with the following teachers in the East Syracuse-Mineola Central Schools to develop this curriculum guide on television viewing skills: Louis DiMento, Lorraine Ellison, Peter Fantinato, Margaret Grindy, Marcia Hayden, Gerald Kelly, James Kelly, Irene Marquart, Robert McGiveny, Peter O'Donnell, Bruno Peutzer, Carl Pulvirenti, Susan Rink, Russell Sager, Suzanne Schaff, Roselynn Shaheen, Donald Thompson, and Noel vanSwol.

Language Arts

Sixth Grade

GENERALIZATIONS Students will be more responsible consumers of goods and services if they are afforded practice in understanding and identifying persuasive elements of commercial messages and given opportunity to produce videotapes of commercial messages of their own. This study, integrated with the existing sixth grade unit, The Language of Symbols, will extend the application of critical thinking skills.

OBJECTIVES
1. Students will learn the meaning and application of propaganda devices such as loaded words, namecalling, slogans, testimonials, image-making, bandwagon technique, and glittering generalities.
2. Students will practice identification of these techniques in printed advertisements before extending practice to reels of outdated commercials donated by a local television channel.
3. Students will analyze commercials with special work/text pages guiding them.
4. Students in small work groups will create a product or service, decide on a target audience, choose an appropriate persuasive device, choose actors and props, and rehearse. When ready, each group will tape a thirty second commercial. When the classwork is screened, the groups will analyze each other's work as they did the professional commercials.

GENERALIZATIONS Students can be helped to an awareness of their personal habits and, through self-understanding, be motivated toward better use of leisure time through more selective television viewing. Further, they can be made aware of the influence of television on the lives of American people and the importance of television to American life.

OBJECTIVES
1. Students will complete detailed diaries of their personal viewing habits with emphasis on self-awareness of their established viewing habits.

Ploghoft and Sheldon

2. Students will compare their eleventh grade diaries with their seventh grade diaries, noting changes in viewing habits.
3. Teachers will confer with students who would like to change their viewing habits.
4. Students will review the importance of television to American life.
5. Students will use argumentative essay skills to write critical essays on television's influence on their lives.
6. Students will distinguish between literary elements in written literature and in television presentations.
7. Students will distinguish between the requirements different media impose upon format.

Twelfth Grade

GENERALIZATION   Students can understand and interpret television news more readily if they are exposed to resource people connected with producing news, take field trips to newspaper offices and television stations, and direct and produce a local, community based news segment.

OBJECTIVES
1. College English students will write Level 2 papers on television's influence as an institution.
2. Other English 12 students will review all areas of television news production, going on field trips whenever necessary.
3. Students will direct and produce a fifteen-minute local news program as a project. Emphasis will be on the community, not solely on the high school.
4. Whenever possible, teachers will provide appropriate resource people to help students with this project.
5. Students will write critiques of one another's projects, emphasizing skills learned in English 2.

Social Studies

GENERALIZATION   Television news is unique in that it offers a montage of action, excitement, and entertainment which the printed news cannot offer. Yet, TV news cannot offer the indepth, wide coverage afforded by the print medium.

Sixth Grade

OBJECTIVES	ACTIVITIES
1. Students will be able to distinguish between local, national, and international news.	1. Given specific news clips, the students will be asked to categorize them.
2. Students will analyze the TV news program to determine the priority given to each news item.	2. Given recorded newscasts, students will determine the importance of each news item based on the time allotted and position given each item in the newscast. Students should: a) List stories in order of presentation. b) Time each news story.
3. Students will compare and contrast the newscasts of three major networks for the content, selection, and emphasis of the day's news.	3. Given videotape of three major newscasts, students will list news items in order of presentation and time allotted to each, stating emphasis of each story. Given the same story as covered by three major networks, students will compare and contrast in terms of time allotted, information stressed, and subjective emphasis.
4. Students will be able to distinguish between objective and subjective news reporting.	4. Given a videotape of a news story, students will be able to recognize the subjective (editorial) emphasis and content.
5. Students will establish their own criterion for local, state, national, and international news.	5. Students will list, in order of importance, the kinds of local, state, national, and international news of which they think the general public should be made aware.
Students will analyze the TV news and compare with their own criteria.	Students will categorize and rank each story on the nightly news and compare the emphasis to their own list.

Ploghoft and Sheldon

6. Students will compare the TV news to reports in newspapers and magazines in terms of content, depth, emphasis, and objectivity.

6. Students will list news items in terms of their importance on a) the front page of the local newspapers and b) the nightly TV news, and discuss differences.
Students will analyze and compare the content and stress of a story as reported in a) the TV news and b) the daily newspaper, and discuss differences.

7. Students will become aware of the process of news gathering on local, state, national, and international levels.

7. Students will take trips to TV stations to become aware of how the news is prepared. Resource people from TV stations will come to talk to students about how the news is prepared. Students will produce a program of school news on videotape.

Twelfth Grade Objectives

1. "To provide youngsters with concepts and skills that enable them to analyze the persuasive messages of commercials, to discriminate between product appeals and affective appeals, and to become sensitive to the subtle persuaders."*
2. "To raise the levels of understanding about the nature and uses of television in the United States."*
3. Given instruction on sociological surveying and sampling techniques, students will be able to gather data, interpret results, and generalize as to the viewing habits of the total population and those of their own peer group.
4. Given appropriate data, students will attempt to analyze the effects of the media on the institution of the family in a television-oriented society with particular emphasis on divorce rates, generation gaps, and the revolution of rising expectations.

* Source: *Abstract*, "An instructional program designed to moderate the effects of television on children and youth," by Milton Ploghoft et al.

GENERALIZATION   Advertisers spend billions of dollars each year promoting their products. Television is a unique vehicle through which millions of potential consumers are exposed to advertising designed specifically to persuade them to purchase particular products.

Twelfth Grade

OBJECTIVES	ACTIVITIES
1. Given statistics on cost of advertising, circulation, and relation of cost to circulation, students will become aware of the impact of TV advertising.	1. Students will compare cost of TV advertising to cost of magazine and newspaper advertising. Students will compare the sizes of audiences reached by TV ads as contrasted to those reached through magazines and newspapers. Students will compare cost of local TV advertising to cost of national advertising.
2. Given a TV commercial, students will tell why it appeals to them (i.e., color, jingle, product).	
3. Given the same commercial, students will discuss the effect of TV commercials as opposed to similar ads in a magazine and the impact of that TV ad.	
4. Students will identify proper techniques used in ads.	
5. Given a commercial, students will analyze proper techniques of that commercial.	
6. Given a certain channel to view on a certain day, students will view what commercials are on, when they are on, and why (audience appeal).	

Ploghoft and Sheldon

7. Students will create their own ads (for the printed media as well as for television).
8. Students will be given instruction on sociological surveying and sampling techniques to gather data and interpret results; they will generalize as to the viewing habits of the total population and those of their own peer group.

English—Television Overview

Sixth Grade

Focus: 1. Commercials.
        bandwagon
        transfer
        testimonial
        loaded words
        slogans
        repetition
    2. News awareness.
    3. Specials.

Seventh Grade

Focus: 1. TV viewing diary.
    2. Choose TV heroes and study their language.
    3. Write an original episode for one hero keeping it in character.
    4. Tour a TV station and take other field trips.
    5. Study TV as an institution.

Eighth Grade

Focus: 1. Commercials.
        symbols
        semantics
        imagination

humor
influence on opinion
2. Create an original commercial.
3. Pick up the idea of heroes again, stressing advertising and touching on entertainment.

Ninth Grade

Focus: 1. TV viewing of entertainment: Analysis of the half-hour series.
2. Compare the literary skills (plot, characterization, theme) in print and on television.

Tenth Grade

Focus: 1. Semantics and language. Using the semantics unit as a basis, discuss bias and slanted reports in news, entertainment, advertising, and public opinion polls.
2. Develop individual projects coming from the unit.
3. Prepare written critical reviews of television.

Eleventh Grade

Focus: 1. Repeat TV viewing diary and compare with the diary kept in seventh grade.
2. Review TV as an institution.
3. Examine critical essays on aspects of TV.
4. Emphasize through videotapes TV characterization and other literary skills; compare the treatment of these skills on TV and in print.

Twelfth Grade

Focus: College prep and freshman English.
1. Review essays on TV as an institution and as an influence on American life.

Focus: Journalism and career English.
1. Review all areas of TV news production.
2. Plan field trips, using resource people in the classroom.
3. Write, direct, and produce a local news program (include sports, weather, commercials).

Situation Comedy—Television Guide

Literal Level

1. What is the major plot line, if any? Does the program depend on multiple subplots? Summarize the plot.
2. What is the setting shown on the TV screen? How does the setting contribute to the plot? Describe any significant or memorable items (props) shown. What external settings are implied?
3. Who are the main characters? How does their appearance (dress) contribute to the characterization?
4. Identify the conflict: Individual vs self; individual vs individual; humankind vs nature; humankind vs God.
5. What is the dominant mood of the story?
6. What type of sitcom is it (career, historical, family, comedy of manners, ideas, intrigue, romance, satire)?
7. What is the pace (slapstick, medium, slow)? Does the pace vary?
8. List the commercials shown before, during, and after the show.
9. Is the show filmed before an audience? Is there a laugh track with it?
10. Is there a musical or pictorial introduction or theme song? Write down any words from the theme or added sound effects that you remember.
11. Identify the level of language the main characters speak (formal, informal, nonstandard). Are there dialects or accents?
12. What are some examples of nonverbal communication used (facial, body)?
13. List camera techniques you noticed.

Interpretive Level

1. Does this show depend more on plot or character?
2. How is the setting related to the plot? How would a different setting change the plot?
3. Which character seems most sympathetic? Which characters are shallow or static? What character stereotypes are included? What human foibles are satirized? Is any character really dynamic?

4. Is the conflict dependent on character, simple plot or both? Is the conflict one of generations, values, sex roles, race, or other factors? Is there inherent conflict in the story line?
5. If the comedy is serious or satirical, is it critical of social conventions? Does it generate attitude changes in the audience, or is the show pure entertainment?
6. Considering the type of sitcom, what attitudes do the writers of the show seem to have toward the situation?
7. How is pace a contribution to humor, social commentary and advancement of plot?
8. What type of audience does this show appeal to (age, location)? Are the commercials aimed at that audience?
9. What effect does the sound track (the added laughter and background sounds) have on the audience? Did you go along with it or resent it?
10. Is the theme music appropriate to the mood of the show? Are lyrics (if any) appropriate? Do the added effects have any special significance?
11. How does the level of language delineate character? What comedy effects do individual accents have? What social class is indicated by the level of language?
12. How do nonverbal communications advance the plot, underscore meaning, add humor, delineate character? How do they let the audience know more than the characters in the show do about reactions and plots? Would it be possible to understand the story without audio?
13. To what extent do camera techniques affect the director's message? Which camera techniques advance the plot? Were any techniques intrusive?
14. Does the show have an overall theme or does it present scattered social commentary (in one-liners)? Is the theme universal or topical? On theme alone, predict the rating or staying power of the program. If the theme is not universal, will the characters carry the show?
15. Does plot, character, or theme carry the show? If the show does not appeal to you, what changes would improve it?
16. If one of a series, is this segment consistent with the philosophy or formula established by previous segments?

Viewer Skills—Sitcom and/or Drama Guide

Laboratory Exercises

1. Summarize the major plot line of a favorite show in ten short sentences. Put each sentence on a separate card. Scramble and then reorganize the cards. Give them to a friend or family member who has not viewed the program.
2. Write a plot of a favorite program viewed with friends. Make a script. Dramatize it. Write a plot with no specific ending. Discuss alternative resolutions with friends and parents.
3. View 90 percent of a program. Leave the room. Write your own ending. Ask someone who viewed it if your ending was similar. Discuss which ending is better and why.
4. Write an original plot line with unique characters. Send it to a network. Ask for response as to acceptability or feasibility?

Setting

1. Research pictures of cars, buildings, and clothes of 1900-1980 in intervals of decades. Imagine futuristic sets.
2. Research the appearance of a mother and a teenager in the same time frames.
3. Which props are needed for a living room and a kitchen for the same time frames?
4. Visit a local TV station. Try to interview prop and makeup personnel. Observe news, weather, and sports sets. Describe your experience to friends.
5. Design a set for local TV, for a program you like, or for a program you'd like to see.

Applied Laboratory Exercises

1. Define: credibility, static, dynamic, hero, stereotype, sympathy, model.
2. Cite examples of these concepts on various TV shows.
3. Interview people whose real-life jobs are depicted in

fictional television programs, police officers, attorneys, reporters, or doctors. Discuss with them the degree of realism and accuracy in the fictional portrayals of their jobs and job-related pressures.

4. Ask a person who is over thirty what the fifties era was really like. Does television exaggerate and artificialize characters' actions, dress, mannerisms, attitudes, or goals?

5. Develop a list of positive characteristics possessed by characters you find a) most likeable, b) most believable, or c) most typical of a person you would like to emulate.

6. Develop a list of negative characteristics possessed by characters whose behavior or philosophy of life you find most undesirable.

7. Compose a monologue or dialogue illustrating your items in questions 5 and 6.

8. Write and dramatize a script involving characters you consistently find real or enjoyable.

9. List your personal goals for the years 1985, 1990, 2000. Match these goals with characters in various TV series who are trying to achieve or have achieved the same or similar goals. Would your methodology be similar? Why?

10. Which characters most clearly resemble you, your family, your friends, your enemies?

11. List the characteristics of persons who would cause you to "turn them off."

Conflict (comic or dramatic)

1. Delineate the type of conflict found in literature and in real life. Apply these to various programs you enjoy. Have you ever rejected a TV program because of too much conflict?

2. Give examples of the following types of conflict as seen in various programs:
   love
   money
   family
   school
   good guys vs bad guys
   male vs female
   race

3. Which conflicts are really important? Give examples of conflict treated humorously. Does this create a counterproductive artificiality?
4. On 3 x 5 cards list characters in No. 2. Switch the characters and conflicts around to create new conflicts. How would you resolve this new conflict? Could a new series be developed? If so, how? What could happen if Archie Bunker met the Fonz?

Advertisements

1. Which ads use a story to sell products?
2. Which ads use the same characters, roles, or stereotypes seen in TV series?
3. Which stars advertise or endorse products? Give examples of those you find believable and unbelievable.

Audience (live, laugh track, home)

1. View programs such as "Celebrity Sweepstakes" and "Family Feud." How is the audience involved in the process of the program rather than as a pool of potential contestants?
2. Which TV shows use laugh tracks and which ones use live audiences? How are they similar and how are they different? Which is more acceptable to you and why?
3. Laugh at an inappropriate time during a comedy show. What will be the reaction of family or friends? Do *not* laugh at situations or lines at which others laugh. Defend your action.
4. Is laughter contagious? When viewing television, do you feel accepted when those around you have reactions similar to yours? Do you feel rejected when your reactions and theirs are dissimilar? Why?
5. Find a TV talk show that accepts phone calls and participate.

Theme song

1. What type of TV series would fit your favorite song?
2. View programs such as "Alice," "All in the Family," "The Jeffersons."

3. Choose a poem you enjoy and adapt it to a theme song about an idea you think is pertinent to your age group. Develop a story to fit the theme song. Send the story script and the taped theme song to a network.

Language (formal, informal, nonstandard, dialect)

1. Which TV shows use dialect to represent Boston? The West? The South?
2. What is the effect of Fonzie's "Aaaay" or Archie Bunker's "Geeeschh"?

Nonverbal communication

1. Watch TV with the sound off for five minutes. What meaning can you get from gestures or body movements alone?
2. Develop a charade or pantomime game involving your favorite characters.

Comparing Situation Comedies

Characterization

1. Which shows have a strong focus on one main character (authority figure, leader, hero)?
2. What are the outstanding traits of the main character?
3. Which main character is most believable? Why? With whom do you identify or sympathize most? Why?
4. Are any main characters stereotypes? Are any unique? Explain.
5. Is any main character more important than the plot (action, dialogue)?
6. How do the characters on each show interact? In which show, if any, does a supporting character get a role equal to or more important than that of the main character?
7. Which shows depend on the same cast of characters each week? Which shows introduce many new characters each week?

Conflict, Plot Development

1. At what point in the shows are the conflicts revealed? How is this done in each show?
2. How believable are the conflicts? Are they trivial or important? Are the conflicts something you might be involved with in real life or are they artificially constructed for the sake of the show and character?
3. Are there any subplots? Which show has the greatest number? Are subplots necessary to develop the main conflicts?
4. What do the subplots add to the comedy of the show?

Resolutions

1. Are any of the shows predictable? Do you have a strong hint from the beginning as to what the resolution will be?
2. Which of the shows have miniclimaxes? Why? In which show were you more aware of them?
3. In which shows are the resolutions convenient endings? Do they follow naturally from the plot or are they contrived?

Humor

1. Would any of the plots be strong (or well-developed) enough to work in formats other than comedy?
2. What types of humor are used in these shows? Which shows depend on the situation for humor; which depend more on language (puns, sarcasm, understatement)? Which are more dependent on slapstick or physical humor? Which are more dependent on facial expressions?
3. Which shows use laugh tracks? Are these laugh tracks effective or offensive?
4. Is the humor in these shows strong enough to stand without a laugh track?

Theme

1. Which shows deal humorously with serious subjects?

2. Does the humorous treatment detract from or add to the serious message?
3. Which shows are intended purely for entertainment?
4. Which shows choose controversial subjects like sex, family problems, or politics?
5. Do any shows deal with moral issues? Identify them.
6. Which shows present a serious subject realistically? How?

Outline for Soap Opera

Characterization

1. What similar types of characters do you find in soap operas?
2. List any stereotypes you notice.
3. Are there any advantages to using stereotypes?
4. Do you find that either sex predominates?
5. If so, which sex is more involved in the major conflicts? Explain.
6. Are any of the major characters allowed to change and develop? Which ones?
7. From what segment(s) of society are most of the characters drawn? What are the levels of education and income of most characters?
8. Are there any exceptions to this? If so, why (for what purpose) are these characters introduced? What happens to them?

Conflict, Plot Development

1. What kinds of conflicts usually appear in any particular show?
2. Are the conflicts primarily of one type, either internal or external?
3. Are the external conflicts usually between two people, or do they involve a large number of characters?
4. Is there more than one major conflict being developed at a given time?
5. Are there subplots? What is the purpose of subplots?
6. Are subplots well developed apart from the main plot(s)?
7. How are openings made in the main plot to allow the introduction of subplots?

Ploghoft and Sheldon

8. Do these subplots seem like natural offshoots or forced situations?
9. Are the plots and conflicts realistic?

Resolution

1. Are most conflicts resolved?
2. Do the resolutions come at appropriate times?
3. If the conflict is drawn out, what are the advantages/disadvantages of this?
4. Does a lengthy conflict or subplot affect the quality or believability of the resolution?
5. How long, on an average, does it take to resolve a conflict?
6. Is there a main climax in each show? When does it occur?
7. Are there miniclimaxes? When? Why?
8. What is the relationship of the miniclimax to the main climax? To the commercials? To the end of the week?

Theme

1. What are the predominant themes common to most soap operas? List them.
2. Which soap operas present themes unique to that particular show?
3. How would you categorize the types of themes used on soap operas as compared to other types of TV shows?
4. How controversial are the themes? Do any of them deal with moral issues? Explain.
5. How do they compare to the treatment of similar themes on prime time television?
6. When a controversial theme is presented, is the intent to inform the viewer or simply to further the plot?

General Evaluation

1. In a paragraph, how would you define or explain a soap opera to someone who had never seen one?
2. For what audience are soap operas intended? Do different programs have different audiences? Explain.
3. List the qualities of soap operas that you think are attractive and appealing to an audience.

4. How would you evaluate the quality of the acting in soap operas?

Television News

Objectives

1. Improve literal listening skills.
2. Determine the tone of news items on daily presentations.
3. Determine the tone and consistency of tone on news specials.
4. Contrast a daily news program with a daily newspaper.
5. Compare and contrast local coverage of news items on the three major networks.
6. Understand the concepts of editorials and editorializing.
7. Compare and contrast local and national editorials on the same subject.
8. Write a letter to the editor reflecting an understanding of an editorial and a reaction to it.
9. Characterize the role assumed by national and local news commentators and analysts.
10. Determine which commentators establish their own biases.
11. Analyze the level of language of various newspersons and attempt to identify the target audience.
12. Analyze commentators' facial expressions and body language as contributors to content.
13. Analyze program commercials and identify the target audiences.
14. Analyze timing and structure of programs in terms of content and impact; identify other dramatic elements such as suspense, comedy, and resolution.

Activities

FIRST WEEK

1. Pretest liberal and applied viewing skills by showing videotape of program followed by liberal questions. Posttest on news items, commercials, timing, tone.
2. Analyze newspaper articles with emphasis on structure of news, editorials, and features. Develop methods of skimming for information and retention. Stress parallels (in form and

information-gathering techniques) between local print news and local broadcast news by showing videotapes of local news broadcasts.

SECOND WEEK

3. Select representative local and national commentators and analysts to determine characteristic body language, facial expression, and role assumed. Analyze content of several editorials on the same subject if possible. Determine the relationship, if any, between role and content.
4. Do the same with "60 Minutes."

THIRD WEEK (culminating written activities—choose 3)

5. Write a letter to the editor reflecting a reaction to an issue discussed on TV or in the newspaper.
6. Analyze one nightly news presentation (local or national) with emphasis on timing, content, commentator's role, editorial bias, and commercials. Discuss reactions in class.
7. Compare and form a judgment as to the effectiveness of television versus newspaper coverage of one specific issue.
8. Categorize and analyze the commercials on any half hour broadcast; determine target audience.
9. Show how any half hour news broadcast is a series of miniature dramas.
10. Develop a teacher-approved, student-designed written activity.

General Television Viewing Guide

1. Identify the characters.
2. Describe the settings—time and place.
3. What is the program about?
4. Identify the types of conflict.
5. Were the conflicts resolved? Were they resolved realistically? Would you resolve the conflicts differently?
6. Give physical descriptions of the characters?
7. List adjectives to describe the characters?
8. How are the characters developed—actions, speech, appearance, gestures, facial expressions?
9. Are the characters adequately developed, or would you classify them as undeveloped, flat, or stereotyped?
10. Are the characters realistic?

11. Do the characters change? If so, is the change prepared for adequately?
12. Does the time length of the show affect characterization and plot development?
13. How do camera angles, camera techniques, and lighting effects help reveal characters?
14. What is the theme of the program? What current events issues are related to the theme?
15. Classify the theme as legal, social, economic, political, or moral.
16. How do music, sound effects, and lighting contribute to the meaning?
17. Classify the program as situation comedy, western, mystery, science fiction, or other.
18. For what age group is the program designed—children, young adults, mature adults?
19. For what age group are the commercials designed? Are the commercials hard sell or soft sell?
20. What propaganda techniques do the commercials use?
21. Are commercials appropriately placed in the program?
22. How well has the program used plot, characterization, camera techniques, and special effects to present its theme?

Social Studies Guide

1. Identify the issues, problems, or conflicts presented in the show.
   legal
   social
   economic
   political
   moral
   religious
2. How does the program present each problem/conflict?
3. What does each person say about the problem?
4. What do individuals do to show how they feel about the problem?
5. With which people do you tend to agree? Why?
6. With which people do you tend to disagree? Why?

Ploghoft and Sheldon

7. What parts of the problem do you feel the show ignored?
8. Does the program stress one side of the problem? How? Was a particular viewpoint or bias stressed? Explain.
9. Does the show resolve the issue or solve the problem? How?
10. How could you solve the problem (in a different way)?
11. What is the moral or lesson of the story? Do you agree with it? Why?

Alternate Discussion Guide

Social Studies

Program _____

Episode Time _____

1. Check the issues presented in the show.

_____ legal   _____ moral

_____ social   _____ religious

_____ economic   _____ other

_____ political

2. How is the problem introduced?

_____ character(s) directly state problem

_____ character(s) indirectly state problem

_____ character(s) suggest problem through actions, gestures, facial expressions

_____ narrator explains problem

_____ situation reveals the problem

3. Identify the main characters and check the statement that reflects your opinion of each character's approach to the problem:

_____ I totally agree with what this character says or implies.

_____ I agree with most of what this character says or implies.

_____ I disagree with much of what this character says or implies.

_____ I totally disagree with what this character says or implies.

4. How was the problem presented? Check **all** statements that apply.

_____ The show presented all sides of the problem.

_____ The show stressed only one side of the problem.

_____ All sides of the problem were shown fairly.

_____ The problem appeared simpler than it really was.

5. What is true of the solution?

_____ The problem was totally resolved.

_____ The problem was only partially resolved.

_____ The solution was suggested or implied.

_____ The solution was left for the audience to decide.

6. What are your personal feelings about the solution to the problem?

_____ I felt satisfied with the solution.

_____ The solution seemed more idealistic than realistic.

_____ The solution seemed real and I was comfortable with it.

_____ The solution seemed ridiculous to me.

_____ The solution seemed real but I wish it hadn't ended that way.

_____ The solution seemed unreal but I liked it.

_____ There was not enough information to suggest a solution.

7. What is true of the lesson(s) or moral(s) of the program?

_____ The lesson/moral was clearly stated.

_____ The lesson/moral was implied.

_____ There was no lesson/moral.

8. Which statements reflect your opinion of the lesson/moral?

_____ The lesson seemed real and I agreed with it.

_____ The lesson seemed real but I disagreed with it.

_____ The lesson did not seem true to life but I agreed with it.

_____ The lesson did not seem true to life and I disagreed with it.

_____ The lesson seemed ideal and I agreed with it.

_____ The lesson seemed ideal and I disagreed with it.

Social Studies Enrichment Questions

Television can take a topic such as war and produce a series that emphasizes different aspects of war. For example, a series such as "M*A*S*H" can emphasize the humorous aspects of war but at the same time have deeper messages for the audience.

1. An important aspect of life near the battlefield is the boredom during periods between emergencies.
   a) After viewing a show about war, explain how the various characters cope with inactivity and frustration.
   b) Can you relate to this search for an escape from boredom?
2. How is "M*A*S*H" a good example of a series that goes beyond the humorous aspects of war? Consider human relationships and the attitudes of the characters in answering this question.
3. Attitudes in America were different during World War II, the Korean War, and the Vietnam War. How does attitude change with the time setting? *Example:* Would the attitudes of army personnel in the Korean setting be different in a World War II setting?
4. "M*A*S*H" and other popular series on war represent an isolated community in microcosm. A wide variety of people who might never come into contact back in the States are forced to live in close proximity with little chance of escape from one another. Write a fifty word character analysis for each major character in "M*A*S*H." Include in your analysis how the characters differ and how their roles affect the series.
5. Why do you watch shows dealing with war plots? Is it because it mirrors your own feelings and experiences or because it is a make-believe world totally unfamiliar to you. Explain.

Reading and Music

Music to Motivate Reluctant Readers

Janet K. Carsetti
READ, Incorporated

Survival in a literate society is the basic premise of Project READ, a national literacy program for troubled youth. Since its inception in 1976, Project READ has worked with more than 40,000 troubled youth from 400 institutions, alternative schools, and community based programs in 50 states and the District of Columbia. Close to one thousand teachers and youth workers have participated in teacher training workshops and more than a quarter of a million paperback books have been distributed to young people across the nation.

Since 1976, Project READ has served five distinct populations:
1. Incarcerated juveniles housed in 148 institutions from 47 states and the District of Columbia.
2. A combination of institutionalized youth from 40 sites previously served, and those from 40 alternative schools and community based programs.
3. Youth in 100 alternative schools and community based programs.
4. Youth from 25 alternative schools, youth shelters, and other community based programs.
5. Approximately 3,000 young people attending four public junior high schools in the District of Columbia.

Since motivation is one of the key elements in reaching reluctant readers, Project READ's efforts have focused on:
- Training teachers who work with troubled youth to use highly motivational techniques such as popular music and functional reading packets.
- Distributing free, high interest paperback books to students.

Music as a Motivational Technique

The universal language of music provides countless hours of listening pleasure. While music listened to is as diversified as are listeners, music plays a role in the lives of most people. For troubled youth, music is a constant companion—provided through portable radios, tape players, and phonographs. Frequently, music is the only form of entertainment these young people have to help pass the time.

Since many young people served by Project READ are deficient in communication skills, music activities are used not only to motivate but also to develop and reinforce listening, reading, and writing skills. Student participation in selecting music to be used is essential to the development of music activities. Student decision making in the learning process can be a tremendous asset. A listening corner may be set up in the classroom with a cassette tape recorder, radio, and/or phonograph. Students may bring in their favorite records and tape them, or they may listen to the radio and record selected songs they know and like. While teachers may not "understand" the words, students may be able to recite them verbatim. Because students are familiar with the words, any listening activities teachers design will be easier for the students.

As teachers read and/or listen carefully to the words of a song, they will discover patterns. For example, some songs have a series of rhyming words or words that begin with the same sound. Some songs lend themselves to categorizing by using words related to food, love, places, people, cities, feelings, colors, or seasons. Teachers may design music activities to reinforce phoneme-grapheme relationships and syllabication principles as well as factual and interpretive listening comprehension skills. The actual activity may be produced in the form of a game or as an activity sheet. Some examples of music activities follow.

Music Bingo

Design an empty "bingo" card that can be easily reproduced. An 8½ x 11 inch piece of paper allows for 25 spaces or squares, five across and five down (see illustration). The middle space can have a picture or "free" sign in it. The card may have a five letter word (such as THINK) across the top row. Once the empty cards are duplicated, any number of students can play. Students will help the teacher complete the activity by filling in their own cards. For example, should the teacher wish to reinforce consonants or blends with a song, s/he will first listen to the words and then list all the words in the song that begin with the consonants or blends. This list becomes the answer key. Next, the consonants and blends are transferred to the bingo cards with one consonant or blend per square. When the teacher is ready to play music bingo, s/he asks the students to fill in their cards with the appropriate letters. Students may look at the flash cards as the teacher says "place the letter *b* in one of the empty boxes on your paper." Random placement of letters is automatic, as each student decides in which boxes to place the letters. Should there be fewer than 24 letters (one box is free), students select any of the letters already on the card and reuse them until all 24 boxes are filled.

Sample card for Music Bingo

Once students have completed their cards they trade papers. Eventually this "trading" will motivate students to make their cards neat and accurate since someone other than they will have to read the card. Once the trading of cards is completed and students familiarize themselves with the letters, they are ready to play music bingo or THINK. The song from which the consonants and blends are taken is played. Remember, this song has been selected by students, so they are familiar with both the words and the music.

As students listen to the song, they listen specifically for words that begin with the consonants and blends on their card. When they hear a word beginning with a consonant, they cross out that letter. As soon as someone crosses out a complete row vertically, horizontally, or diagonally, the person yells "THINK." At this time, the teacher may ask the winner which letters have been crossed out and which words in the song begin with those letters. Others may help match words and letters if the winner has forgotten. A prize given to the winner may add to the excitement and motivation of this game. Prizes for students in Project READ schools have included paperback books, candy, gum, or points.

The same song may be played more than once. After the first winner is selected, students may continue listening for the letters in the four corners of their card until they have crossed out all the letters on their card for "blackout bingo." Music bingo can be used with fast, slow, or moderate music. However, if students are having a difficult time hearing words and locating letters, teachers should begin with slower music and build up to a faster pace.

Variations of this game are achieved by changing the skill and/or the size of the card. Younger or slower students may need a nine-box card, with three boxes across and three down. This, of course, limits the number of letters one has to find. One card may use only consonants while another may use only blends. A real challenge is provided by writing complete words in the boxes. When listening to a song, students listen for words with either the same or opposite meanings. When using this more challenging activity, it is recommended that students work in pairs. Music bingo has been used successfully with all age groups and with a variety of songs.

Rhyming Activities

Many songs employ the use of rhyming. Listening for words that end with the same sound is a good reinforcement activity for the skill of rhyming. Teachers may wish to provide the word endings in writing for students having difficulty in recognizing rhyming patterns. Students are then prepared to listen for specific endings.

Clozure

As with any reading selection, a listening activity may require purpose setting in the form of preparation before the selection is heard. An activity sheet using cloze can prepare students for what they are about to hear. Several sentences from a popular song are written with key words omitted. Students listen for the missing words and then complete the sentences.

Vocabulary Development

Matching activities can be used after listening to a song. Lists of synonyms and antonyms and lists of words with definitions may be matched.

Interpretive Thinking

Many songs proclaim statements and feelings on issues such as war, drugs, love, death, and hate. After listening to a song with a message, students may be asked to take issue with the artists' feelings through discussion or by writing.

Category words about people, places, foods, and colors, frequently can be heard in a song. Students can be divided into teams, with each team assigned to listen for a specific category.

Other songs may be used to stimulate creative writing and poetry. Rewriting songs can be motivational for some students when they are asked to replace the nouns in a song with people and places from their own experiences. Similarly, verbs may be changed, or all descriptive words can be changed to express opposite meanings.

The extent to which music activities can be used in the classroom is infinite. Whether used as a stimulator for creative writing or as a means to reinforce consonants, music can motivate the most reluctant learners.

Using Music As a Teaching Tool

Sarina Simon
Los Angeles, California

Can you name three songs from the "Top Ten" list? Your students can! They can also recite and compare the lyrics, summarize the themes, anticipate the outcomes, defend their favorite songs, and make value judgments.

Want proof? Take half an hour with your students to discuss three Top Ten songs. You'll be amazed. The same students who can't identify rhyming words or summarize main ideas in a reading lesson, probably will contribute as enthusiastically and capably as your most advanced readers.

The purpose of this article is to suggest ways in which we, as educators, can take this marvelous, self-taught ability and use it to improve comprehension skills, just as we use all the other knowledge students bring with them to school. Use this ability not as a reward, enrichment, or as busy work but as a motivating, valuable teaching tool. What is the difference, after all, between understanding the printed and the spoken word? After decoding skills are mastered, is it really more difficult to understand what you read than what you hear? On the contrary, fluent readers may find it easier to get meaning from print than from listening to a speaker or a song.

In the past ten years, teachers and scholars alike have placed tremendous emphasis on decoding skills. Nationwide reading scores reflect this emphasis: Word identification scores *have* improved, but comprehension scores have gone down. Put simply, we're teaching students to read words, but students don't understand what they are reading. Something has gone wrong.

Am I suggesting that understanding Shakespeare, or even a story in a basal reader, involves the same skills as understanding the

Rolling Stones? No. But then again, yes.

My interest in popular music as a teaching tool has not impaired my critical faculties. Bob Dylan is not Chaucer. Carole King is no Edna St. Vincent Millay. But contemporary artists do write a kind of poetry, and their poetry can be used to help students understand the beauty, meaning, and relevance of outstanding poetry.

James Brown, the soul singer, is not likely to be mistaken for James Baldwin. Surely Loretta Lynn would wonder at being compared with Virginia Woolf. Yet, these four people all have something in common. When Brown sings, "Say it loud—I'm Black and I'm proud," and when Lynn sings, "The Games that Daddies Play," they are addressing themselves to contemporary social issues. These songs may not approach the depth of their literary counterparts, but they can be used to introduce or reinforce reading.

Examples such as these abound. In the following pages I shall suggest several teaching strategies and provide a discography for those who are willing to take the plunge.

One last point: As you read through the teaching strategies, you will notice I have suggested several which do not relate directly to comprehension. The reason for this is simple. Music, like literacy, has many dimensions and each is worth teaching.

Teaching Strategies

I. Specific Skill Reinforcement: Main Idea, Sequence

Provide students with parallel listening/reading activities. The success of this strategy will depend on how closely the listening activity parallels the reading activity. The reading activity will be most effective if it is assigned immediately after completion of the listening activity. Proceed in the following manner:

    a. Choose a song which suits your needs.

    b. Tell students that you are going to play a record for them. Ask them to pay special attention to the lyrics. Tell them you are going to ask them afterwards to summarize the song and to distinguish between real and make-believe. (The specific directions will depend on the skill you wish to teach.)

    c. Play the record. Ask questions which relate to the specific skill you are teaching. If necessary, repeat the process with the same record or with several different records.

    d. Present the students with a short passage. Explain that you will be asking them the same kinds of questions you asked about the record. Have students read the passage and answer related questions orally or in writing.

2. Poetry, Essays, Short Stories
Several useful approaches are possible:

   a. Use the musical selections as introductions to a specific theme.
   Example
   Theme   Interference in the course of love.
   Literary Selection   "Romeo and Juliet"
   Musical Selections   "A Boy Like That" (*West Side Story* soundtrack); "Just Like Romeo and Juliet" (recording by The Reflections); "Brother Louie" (recorded by Stories).

   b. Use the musical selections to discuss poetry, specifically meter, rhyme, and free verse.
   Example
   Literary Selection   Any appropriate work.
   Musical Selections   Here, too, almost any song will prove appropriate; for free verse examples, consider early Bob Dylan.

   c. Use the musical selections to portray contrasting viewpoints.
   Example
   Theme   War.
   Literary Selection   Any appropriate short story or essay.
   Musical Selections   "The Universal Soldier" (Tim Hardin, Buffy St. Marie); "War" (recording by Edwin Starr); "The Green Berets" (recording by Barry Sadler).

3. Use musical selections to suggest creative writing and essay themes.
   Example
   Theme   School.
   Musical Selections   "Don't be a Dropout" (James Brown); "The Class of '57" (Statler Brothers); "Be True to Your School" (Beach Boys); "Kodachrome" (Paul Simon).

4. Use Musical selections to introduce the study of a historical era.
   Example
   Theme   The 60s—Youth in Turmoil.
   Musical Selections   "Four Dead in Ohio" (Crosby, Stills, Nash); "Woodstock" (Joanie Mitchell); "For What It's Worth" (Buffalo Springfield).

The following discography is organized by broad thematic categories. A wide variety of musical materials is listed in each: pop songs, country-western, rhythm and blues, show tunes, and oldies. Each song title is listed along with the name of the artist and record label.

Because of the fluid nature of popular music, today's hit is tomorrow's anachronism. Therefore, any discography is mainly a guide to the past. For a guide to the most current songs (the top ten hits to which your students know all the words), consult your local top forty radio station.

DISCOGRAPHY

CATEGORY "Loneliness"

Are You Lonesome Tonight?	Elvis Presley	RCA
I'm So Lonesome I Could Cry	Hank Wiliams	MGM
In My Room	Beach Boys	Capitol
Don't Let Me Be Lonely Tonight	James Taylor	Warner
Empty Bed Blues	Bessie Smith	Columbia
Last Dance	Donna Summer	Casablanca

CATEGORY "School"

Beauty School Dropout	GREASE soundtrack	RSO
Don't Be a Dropout	James Brown	King
Be True to Your School	Beach Boys	Capitol
Status Back Baby	Mothers of Invention	Verve
Charlie Brown	Coasters	Atlantic
You've Got to Be Taught	SOUTH PACIFIC soundtrack	MGM
School Days	Chuck Berry	Chess
Harper Valley PTA	Jeannie C. Riley	RCA

CATEGORY "Urban Life"

Summer in the City	Lovin' Spoonful	Kama Sutra
Hot Child in the City	Nick Glider	Chrysalis
59th Street Bridge Song	Simon & Garfunkel	Columbia
Detroit City	Bob Luman	RCA
Up on the Roof	Drifters	Atlantic
There's No Pity (in the Naked City)	Jackie Wilson	Brunswick

CATEGORY "Rural Life"

Coal Miner's Daughter	Loretta Lynn	MCA
Lukenback Texas	Waylon Jennings	RCA
Blue Bayou	Linda Ronstadt	Asylum
Oklahoma!	OKLAHOMA soundtrack	RCA
Sweet Home Alabama	Lynyrd Skynyrd	Warner
Goin' Up Country	Canned Heat	UA
Country Roads	John Denver	RCA

CATEGORY "Love" (saying "I Love You")

Peggy Sue	Buddy Holly	Coral
Lovely Rita	Beatles	Capitol
3 Times a Lady	Commodores	Motown
Love is the Foundation	Loretta Lynn	MCA
Tonight	WEST SIDE STORY soundtrack	Columbia
You Needed Me	Anne Murray	Capitol

CATEGORY "Summer"

Summer Nights	GREASE soundtrack	RSO
Hot Fun in the Summertime	Sly & the Family Stone	Columbia
Summertime	Jamies	Swan
See You in September	Happenings	
Summertime Blues	The Who	MCA
Summer in the City	Lovin' Spoonful	Kama Sutra

CATEGORY "Unrequited Love"

Hopelessly Devoted	Olivia Newton-John	RSO
Before the Next Teardrop Falls	Freddy Fender	ABC
You Won't See Me	Beatles	Capitol
It Doesn't Matter Anymore	Buddy Holly	Coral
You Really Got a Hold on Me	The Miracles	Tamla
Since I Fell for You	Lenny Welch	

CATEGORY "War"

Universal Soldier	Tim Hardin	Folkways
Blowin' in the Wind	Peter, Paul, & Mary	Warner
Masters of War	Bob Dylan	Columbia
Battle of New Orleans	Johnny Horton	Columbia
Ballad of the Green Berets	Barry Sadler	
War	Edwin Starr	Motown

CATEGORY "Marriage"

Matchmaker	FIDDLER ON THE ROOF soundtrack	RCA
Makin' Whoopee	Ray Charles	ABC
Wedding Bells	Hank Williams	MGM
I'm Gonna Get Married	Lloyd Price	Trip
Chapel of Love	Dixie Cups	Soma
Love and Marriage	Doris Day	Columbia

CATEGORY "Breaking Up"

D-I-V-O-R-C-E	Tammy Wynette	RCA
Breaking Up is Hard to Do	Neil Sedaka	
You Don't Bring Me Flowers	Streisand/Diamond	Columbia
You Beat Me to the Punch	Mary Wells	Motown
Where Did Our Love Go?	Supremes	Motown
I'm Gonna Wash that Man Right Outa My Hair	SOUTH PACIFIC soundtrack	MGM
Don't It Make My Brown Eyes Blue?	Crystal Gayle	UA

CATEGORY "Social Commentary"

Society's Child/At Seventeen	Janis Ian	Columbia
Celluloid Heroes	Kinks	RCA
Take This Job and Shove It	Johnny Paycheck	Columbia/Epic
Look at Me, I'm Sandra Dee	GREASE Soundtrack	RSO
American Pie	Don McLean	UA
Games that Daddies Play	Loretta Lynn	MCA
Ball of Confusion	Temptations	Motown

Folsom Prison Blues	Johnny Cash	Columbia
America	WEST SIDE STORY soundtrack	Columbia
I'm Black and I'm Proud	James Brown	King
Will You Still Love Me Tomorrow?	Shirelles	Scepter

CATEGORY "Love Lost"

Sandy	GREASE soundtrack	RSO
You Don't Know What You've Got Till You Lose It	Ray Donner	Roulette
Lonely Teardrops	Jackie Wilson	Brunswick
There Goes My Baby	Drifters	Atlantic
Tragedy	Fleetwoods	Dolton
It's Over	Roy Orbison	Monument
There's Still Someone I Can't Forget	Charley Pride	RCA
This Nearly Was Mine	SOUTH PACIFIC soundtrack	RCA
Tears on My Pillow	GREASE soundtrack	RSO

Teaching Reading through Music: Literacy with a Plus

Olive R. Francks
Fordham University at Lincoln Center

The current popularity of the "back to basics" movement has made it especially important that serious attention also be given to the essential role of the arts in our daily curriculum. Although the concept of literacy is generally restricted to achievement in the 3 Rs, this concept should be extended to embrace the arts as bodies of knowledge and forms of human intelligence that are basic to the educative process. This particular aspect of literacy is frequently referred to as "artistic literacy." The artistic dimension describes more than skills, for it goes straight to the heart of thought and feeling and, as such, deserves a central place in educational priorities, including reading.

As teachers and administrators, we seek not only to share with our students our fund of accumulated knowledge, but also to allow them the chance to express what Hughes Mearns called "the voice of the individual spirit." This implies a perception of literacy as something far beyond the mere mastery of the ordinary skills and drills assigned in teaching reading. This literacy includes space for inner thoughts, feelings, visions and values, through artistic modes of knowing and communicating.

In the Beginning Is the Art Form

Would you like to implement an arts and reading approach in your classroom or school? It is a good idea to begin with one art form with which you feel at ease. Ask yourself, "What art form have I ever studied; do I have a particular interest in it? Would I like to study it?"

Your answers will help focus your teaching plans for the beginning stages of a reading-through-the-arts approach. Theater interests include every art form imaginable: painting, music, ballet, modern dance, sculpture, photography, crafts, stained glass, quilt-making, pottery, miniatures, embroidery. Taken at random, the level of knowledge and skill in any group of teachers or administrators will stretch from that of the untrained novice to the advanced creative and performing abilities of the professional artist.

A basic assumption which underlies a reading-through-the-arts approach is that artistic knowledge, skills, and understanding can be taught. The classroom teacher or school supervisor who has the interest, sense of openness, and willingness to try something novel, can be successful. Of course, not all individuals are equally endowed with artistic genius. Within limitations, however, there is far more opportunity for artistic growth and awareness than most adults realize. For many, the greatest obstacle seems to lie in underestimating one's own artistic talents. Indeed, such an attitude is pervasive among adults in our society and is too easily transmitted to young people. The arts, like reading, can be learned and improved upon in our daily lives through intelligent practice, personal commitment, and actual first-hand or "hands-on" experiences which involve the learner in making, creating, and performing, set in a context of accepting the risk of making an occasional mistake.

A Guide to This Approach

The following suggestions for linking the arts with reading are meant to be guides, rather than a prescribed series of steps in initiating this approach in your classroom. The art form being presented here is music; however, the same ideas and procedures may be applied to any other art form.

First, select an art form that appeals to you, or with which you have had a happy familiarity sometime in your life. Whether you play a musical instrument or have attended concerts, opera, or other live musical performances in recent months, you have the capacity to listen attentively to music as well as the ability to operate a phonograph or tape recorder. Therefore, you now have at your fingertips endless possibilities for musical study and enjoyment, and for integration with reading and language learning in your classroom or school.

Next, you should be ready to begin wherever you are, in terms of knowledge, skills, and sensitivity to the art form itself. Encourage your students through your own example and attitude. If you are attracted to symphonic, operatic, choral, or chamber music in a special way, you should begin to develop a clear and disciplined understanding of some of the major composers, performing artists, and recordings, so that you will be at ease in playing these for others. Until you do gain a sense of comfort with these, you might confine your teaching in the classroom to listening to music in more passive ways, such as using background music while reading, writing, or thinking.

Teaching Comparison as a Reading Skill

Musical compositions, although created for aesthetic purposes, may also serve in reading and language learning at a different level of knowing. For example, you may plan to focus on ways by which ideas can be compared or contrasted in order to help youngsters see relationships among facts, generalizations, values, and feelings. In such an instance, the class would read a passage such as the one in which two cities are described: A very old city, and one which is ultramodern (Karlin, 1977). You will then help the children to name and list the differences they have noted in the two descriptive passages. This activity may be written on the chalkboard or a permanent chart or worksheet, as suggested in the following material:

A VERY OLD CITY	AN ULTRAMODERN CITY
In a very old city, we would be likely to find:	Here, we would probably find:
1. Buildings made of stone or brick.	1. Buildings made of glass, steel, concrete.
2. Narrow cobblestone or unpaved paths and ways.	2. Wide streets and avenues, paved and smooth.
3. Small, one- or two-story houses and shops.	3. Tall skyscrapers reaching 100 stories or more and huge department stores.
4. Businesses and houses close together, easy to get to without cars or buses.	4. Everything really vast and spread out at distances, so you need transportation to get there.
5. Antique lampposts, lighting, and signs.	5. Brightly lit signs, ads, billboards, and discotheques.

Comparisons and Contrasts in Reading Materials

In order to compare objects or ideas, children learn to look at these as being either the same, different, related, or opposed to the other(s) being compared. Questions which may be asked include the following: "How is _____ like _____?" "Is _____ the same (different) as (from) _____?" "Why or why not?" "What makes _____ seem to be related to _____?"

Teaching the Same Skills

Using Music Instead of Printed Text

The same skills may be taught and applied in different contexts. Instead of using printed passages, the skill of comparison can be taught through passages selected from musical compositions. The musical theme, "Storms," is used here as a model which can be adapted to your own circumstances:

> a. Beethoven's "Country Storm" from the Third Movement of his Symphony No. 6, *The Pastoral*, can be listened to, discussed, and later compared to
>
> b. Mendelssohn's "Storm at Sea," from his *Hebrides Overture*.

After the children have listened to each musical storm theme, you may wish to ask questions similar to those used in the preceding example about city environments. For example: What are some differences which you perceived between the two storms we listened to? Which of these storms affected you more? In what ways? Why? How do you feel about being in the country in a storm (Beethoven's "Country Storm Theme")? How would you feel about being on the sea during a great storm (Mendelssohn's "Storm at Sea Theme")? What did you "see" in your mind's eye as you listened to this musical theme? Compare the two themes in words, in paint, in body movement.

Contrasting Two Ideas

Using Musical Themes

Continuing the same technique used in teaching comparison, to teach contrast, you may now consider two peaceful and idyllic musical themes such as the following:

> a. Handel's "Pastorale" from his oratorio, *The Messiah*.
> b. Grieg's "Morning" from his *Peer Gynt Suite*.

Each of the listed musical themes is familiar to many youngsters. Contrast the gentle, languorous, softly moving themes with the two previously discussed storm themes. Without describing the music beforehand to the children, play a recording of one of the storm themes and follow this with one of the quieter pastoral themes. A few questions which you may want to build upon include: Which expresses the way you feel today? If you had a choice, in which of these settings would you like to be at this moment—stormy or tranquil? Why? Contrast your feelings as you become part of the music. What does it mean to make contrasts as experienced through *musical* passages instead of those in print?

Unobtrusively, the teacher will record the children's thoughts and feelings as they are expressed during the lesson. As a collective, descriptive story account of each of the musical comparisons, the spoken responses may be captured in a variety of ways. One of the most direct ways uses a structure for organizing children's thinking, as follows:

STORMY MUSICAL THEMES	TRANQUIL MUSICAL THEMES
We heard *The Hebrides Overture*.	We heard "Morning" from the *Peer Gynt Suite*.
Composer: Felix Mendelssohn.	*Composer*: Edward Grieg.
Musical description: lapping of waves against the shore; rough weather, wind, and sea; heavy surf near a cave by the shore; Scottish melodies keep moving!	*Musical description*: soft, easy melodies; flowing, floating along; just waking from a dream; daydreaming again; relaxing in a meadow; happy days in the country, shhhhhhhh!

Using the preceding descriptions as a structure for writing and reading, ask the children to help you prepare reading material similar to that in a good story or tradebook. These stories may also be used for group and individual reading when finished, and because of their personal meaning to the youngsters, will be read and reread for study and for enjoyment many times over.

Alternatives

Nonclassical Music

Nonclassical forms of music also may be used in ways similar to those described here. For a comparison of singers' styles, children will compare one popular vocalist or group with another. A few vocalists and groups are cited below. Make your own choices, however, based upon your own and your students' interests and preferences.

Peter Frampton	The Bee Gees
Carly Simon	The Rolling Stones
Diana Ross	The Beatles
Jackson Brown	Led Zeppelin

Questions similar in form to those asked in previous examples can be developed in the following ways: What do these singers/groups have in common? What is special to each?

Next, select one vocalist/group and, by playing recordings from different periods in their careers, trace how the group evolved over the years. Try this technique by playing selections from records of great vocalists such as Ray Charles, Aretha Franklin, Elvis Presley, and Frank Sinatra. Listen, compare, evaluate. Compare and contrast the vocabularies used in each recording, the meanings evoked by the lyrics and music, and the expressive styles of the vocalists.

A More Sophisticated Choice of Music

It has been shown that through a brief study of certain musical themes and ideas, and by children's individual and collective reactions, the skills of critical evaluation may be practiced in the meaningful context of music as well as in the more traditional printed passage. The musical experience involves a dimension which includes, rather than excludes, the learners' responses and feelings. The music selected for this purpose does not have to fit into each child's past experiences; the wordless, nonverbal ideas, images, and feelings which surface in listening to the music are intrinsically part of children's lives and inner experiences. The typical reading lesson often overlooks this fact by neglecting to touch upon the child's inner life of feeling.

The teacher's own appraisal of pupils' capacities to listen attentively and actively is a better guide in determining the length of a composition to be played than a mandated listing of musical compositions arranged according to age or grade level. Some youngsters are able to listen with care for long periods of time, while others may find ten minutes to be long enough. Many students (including younger children) tend to tune in and out—whether it be to the sound of music, random noise, or conversation—and then to pick up the musical "thread" once again after a few brief intervals have passed. For these reasons, the habits and skills of listening to music may need to be taught directly until they have been internalized. This fact, however, should not deter the teacher from making a more sophisticated choice of musical recordings for class enjoyment and appreciation.

In his distinguished work with children and youth in the area of creative arts, Mearns (1958) once commented that, "Rich artistry among children is simply universal." Age and/or stages of development appear to have little to do with the capacity for delight and neither do socioeconomic status, grade level, achievement scores, nor the many labels often attached to children in our educational world. Even the youngest child, when given a proper chance, will respond sensitively to the music of great composers—Palestrina, Beethoven, Strauss, Prokofieff, or Cage—and should never be limited solely to a musical diet of finger plays and one-line songs.

Reviewing a Musical Work

The 1812 Overture

The next few samples of children's work were done by a group of fourth graders in an urban metropolitan public school. These represented three individual reactions to Tschaikowsky's *1812 Overture*. Each was written originally as a music review, in a format similar to a book review. Each youngster listened, contemplated what the music was saying, then wrote a review, giving an original title and a short story about the musical message, including what the sounds might have meant.

MUSICAL COMPOSITION: THE 1812 OVERTURE
Peter Ilytch Tschaikowsky

1. Sharon's Music Review
   Title: "God of the Seasons"
   Story: It was a rainy night that Crocus, the King of Thunder, threw lightning. Then the god of spring threw flowers and the trees bloomed.
   Sounds: It sounded like a giant stepping on a house.

2. Eddie's Music Review
   Title: "The Chase"
   Story: The hunters search for game. They spot it. They chase it and tromp through the pond and through the forest. They jump over banks. They lose it, but then they load their guns. Fire! And they hit the animal.
   Sounds: One of the sounds sounded like a trumpet.

3. Sonja's Music Review
   Title: "Coming of Danger"
   Story: Going to war. Getting closer to victory. We begin to lose. Then victory is near and, at last, peace is here. A celebration!
   Sounds: I hear stampeding of horses and people dancing.

The teacher may also choose freer forms of writing for some youngsters, helping them to express their ideas poetically with less rigid structure and format than in the preceding reviews. Using Sharon's and Sonja's ideas, the teacher asked both children to work together on a simple collaborative poem:

LISTENING

It was a rainy night and dark
When Crocus, King of Thunder,
Threw lightning bolts around the sky
And trees and flowers bloomed
As the god of spring came by.

From the many thoughts about the sounds heard in the *1812 Overture*, the children were also asked to sharpen their poetic ideas, selecting only those images which strengthened the poetic concept they had in mind. The first of the music reviews was reset into a little poetic fragment which begins in this way:

Into the dark and rainy sky
Rose Crocus, King of Thunder
Throwing his arrows of lightning
To crash in an eye of the storm....

To Call Forth the Spirit of Artistic Literacy

Music and reading make good companions, supportive of each other and of the learner. Each provides a message with or without words, calling upon individual students to interpret the meaning for themselves. To be literate in our culture should require far more than decoding and word recognition skills; literacy implies the ability to think, to encode, to interpret, to evaluate, to be able to manipulate a variety of codes and symbols. Dewey (1934) ascribed the role of intelligence in artistic work in the following way:

> To think effectively in terms of relations of qualities is as severe a demand upon thought as to think in terms of symbols, verbal and mathematical. Indeed, since words are easily manipulated in mechanical ways, the production of a work of genuine art probably demands more intelligence than does most of the so-called thinking that goes on among those who pride themselves as being intellectuals.

The arts, seen within this framework, should be included in any concept of literacy which purports to describe the educated person in our society, i.e., one who is able to think with clarity and openness, who is accepting of new and steady visions, and who can, when needed, march to a different drummer. Reading and the arts offer one avenue of approach into that fuller, more gracious view of literacy which exists beyond the basics.

References

Allinson, A., et al. *Multiworlds guidebook*. Glendale, California: Bowmar, 1973.

Chenfield, M. *Teaching language arts creatively*. New York: Harcourt Brace Jovanovich, 1978.

Dewey, J. *Art as experience*. New York: Minton, Balch, 1934.

Eisner, E. Arts curricula for the gifted. *Teachers College Record*, 1966, *67*, 492-501.

Francks, O.R. Literacy and meaning in the arts. *Learning Center Reports*, 1976, *2*, 24-30. Fordham University School of Education and Community School District.

Gardner, H. Promising paths toward artistic knowledge: A report from Harvard Project Zero. *Journal of Aesthetic Education*, 1976, *10*, 201-207.

Karlin, R. *Teaching elementary reading*. New York: Harcourt Brace Jovanovich, 1977.

Knieter, G.L. Musicality is universal. *Teachers College Record*, 1966, *67*, 485-491.

Mearns, H. *Creative power: The education of youth in the creative arts*. New York: Dover, 1958.

Mursell, J.L. *Developmental teaching*. New York: McGraw-Hill, 1949.

Rico, G.L. *Reading for nonliteral meaning*. In Elliot Eisner (Ed.), *Reading, the arts, and the creation of meaning*. Reston, Virginia: National Art Education Association, 1978, 33-53.

Zintz, M. *The reading process: The teacher and the learner* (2nd ed.). Dubuque, Iowa: Wm. C. Brown, 1975.

Reading and the Graphic Arts

Developing Reading Skills
through the Study of Great Art

Elizabeth H. Rowell
Rhode Island College

Have you ever noticed now many famous artists have painted pictures of human figures reading? Painters such as El Greco, Gauguin, van Gogh, Degas, Rembrandt, Copley, Picasso, Cassatt, Fragonard, Cezanne, Toulouse-Lautrec, Durer, and Renoir have illustrated the importance of reading in their works. Artists have shown that it is possible to combine the communication of art and reading for an aesthetic experience. But it is also possible to combine a study of great art and correlated reading activities to better equip students to deal with the printed word.

How can a painting of a bowl of sunflowers or a portrait of two clowns and a dog help students to learn to read? Art works and reading materials are really very much alike and the understanding process for both is very similar. Pictures and print are both meant to be looked at with the eye as well as with the mind.

Our eyes see only the surface—the words on a page of print or the lines, colors, shapes, and subjects of a painting. But when our minds help our eyes to interpret a page of print or a painting, we begin to understand as well as see. To comprehend what we have and to appreciate art, we must take someone else's recorded experiences, feelings, imagination, and thoughts, expressed through an art medium or through printed words, and understand them in light of our own personal feelings and knowledge. As we are learning to understand and appreciate art, we are at the same time working on processes that are also necessary to fully comprehend printed matter.

The combination of art and print is seen everywhere in our society. Art works abound in texts and trade books, ranging from preprimers and picture books through subject area books at high school and college levels. A combination of art and printed words in the form of advertisements that appear in magazines, newspapers, on billboards, and TV is used to urge us to purchase goods and services. It is assumed that people in our society both notice and react to the combination of print and pictures they encounter daily.

Just as a book about art or an intriguing illustration in a book can sometimes awaken a student's interest in art, so can an interest in art often awaken and stimulate a student's interest in reading.

A study of famous paintings can be used to develop some of the basic reading skills as well as to create an interest in art. Students can improve their reading and become more aware of art in their lives by strengthening their visual and perceptual skills while looking at art, acquiring new concepts and vocabulary as they read and study about art. Gradually they learn to go from understanding more realistic and concrete pictures and ideas to the more symbolic and abstract as they discuss and write about art.

Most students like art, and a demanding study of a complex skill such as reading needs a variety of activities to make the task enjoyable. Extra time spent in reading pays off in increased growth in skills and interest, so why not teach some basic reading skills while students are learning to enjoy and understand great art? It is possible to open the worlds of both art and reading to students through art appreciation.

This article suggests some ideas for turning every classroom into a mini art gallery to help students increase their reading powers as they increase their abilities to enjoy and appreciate art.

Starting Out

When using art forms to teach basic reading skills, first get the students hooked on art by starting at their interest and knowledge levels. Some youngsters come to school from homes where art works abound, and they have begun to appreciate and understand different types of art. But many students have not been exposed to art work nor have they had the opportunity to visit museums or galleries. These students may have developed their own narrow understanding and appreciation standards. For example, some students like only pictures in which the color red is dominant. If a picture contains a lot of red, it is "great." Other students may cherish any painting that features dogs, but think paintings of people are "stupid" or "boring." Some may like realistic paintings, but will not try to understand or enjoy abstract art.

Just as reading interest inventories are often given to determine the kinds of books to include in the classroom library, it is often helpful to administer an art interest inventory to ascertain which types of art interest students. This can be accomplished easily by showing students a variety of pictures which often appeal to youngsters of similar ages—animals, children, nature, clowns, or pop art—to find out which ones they like and why. Works by van Gogh, Seurat, Gauguin, Chagall, Klee, Matisse, and Manet seem to appeal to most beginning art connoisseurs.

Start with the types of pictures that interest most of the students, and then gradually expand their artistic horizons and introduce them to the works of other artists such as Miro, Rembrandt, Picasso, and Wyeth. Encourage students to take enough time to really look at a painting. As one seven year old said, "You can see a lot more if you keep looking at it." At first, while an appreciation for art is being kindled, let the students freely discuss and write about their own interpretations and feelings. Gradually, they can be introduced to new art terms and concepts.

Illustrations in Children's Books

Some children's books with good art work may serve to arouse interest in art with younger children. Illustrations have been an important part of children's books for many years and, due to modern printing techniques, better art is now available in these books. Such illustrations are usually created especially for children and are found in the meaningful context of a story so that the children will have a common background to use while interpreting them.

When pictures in carefully selected children's books are used to stimulate students' interest in art, youngsters can begin to see that pictures are not only a way of enhancing a story, but are also something to be valued and appreciated for their own sake. After reading a book illustrated by Maurice Sendak, Leo Lionni, Robert McCloskey, or Celestino Platti, ask the students if they can find and recognize the artist's work in other books. What makes their illustrations different and easy to recognize? What techniques did the artist use—collage? water colors? oils? charcoal? What colors occur frequently?

Students can learn more about their favorite illustrators through information found in books such as the series of *Illustrators of Children's Books* (published by Horn Book) covering different periods from 1744 to the present. Biographical data and pictures of illustrators may also be obtained from school or town librarians who often keep files on children's illustrators, or by writing to publishers. Although the materials may be difficult for young children to read themselves, teachers could use this information to read to the students to tell them more about the artists, or to write brief, easy-to-read biographical sketches that the students could read for themselves. Some students have written to their favorite illustrators and received personal replies, including personal anecdotes that have helped the students to better understand and appreciate the work of the artist. It is also sometimes possible to get illustrators to speak at school programs. This is another incentive for students to try their own hand at illustrating a story or poem and has interesting long range implications for future career education and vocational choices.

Students can read the text and look at illustrations in books that were awarded the Caldecott Medal for the illustrator of the most distinguished American book for children. Students can carefully study all of the nominees for a certain year, choose their own award winners, and give reasons for their choices. They may or may not agree with the expert judges, but this activity will probably stimulate them to look more carefully at illustrations in the future.

Calling students' attention to the various types of illustrations in books can help them to better appreciate both art and literature. In some instances, artists might differ on their illustrations for the same story. After the students are familiar with a story, such as *Little Red Riding Hood* or *Snow White*, bring in several editions of these tales illustrated by different artists. Ask the students to concentrate on the pictures. How are the pictures similar or different? Which do they think best illustrate the story and why?

Many content area texts contain reproductions of famous art. These, as well as selected prints that tie in with the subject matter, can be used for older students as possible initiating points of understanding. Older students are often intrigued by the works of contemporary artists such as Klee, Dali, and Wyeth or works of the new pop artists including Lichtenstein, Oldenburg, and Wesselmann.

It is very easy to turn an ordinary classroom into a mini art gallery and help students learn to enjoy and appreciate art by living with it. Prominently display pictures and art objects for visual appreciation. This will provide a common ground for discussion and can serve as an incentive to read. A few well chosen, interestingly displayed items on a

"Great Art" bulletin board or in a "Beauty Corner" or in a "Reading and Art" interest center are usually noticed, especially when they are changed frequently. Attention can be directed to the art works by having a "Painting of the Week" (or month or semester) contest in which students select the class favorite from a number of selections. Through discussion and analyses of well-known artists and their works, students may become interested in and familiar with art, and at the same time increase their abilities to visualize, verbalize, analyze, and interpret their personal feelings about art.

Guest Speakers in the Classroom

Local artists, art historians, museum guides, volunteers, and amateur and professional painters can be invited to display, demonstrate, and discuss art work. A visit to a nearby art gallery or private collection might add to students' interest in art. Some museums may send representatives to talk with students before they visit the museums. These talks usually include the showing of slides and other materials to prepare the students for what they will see on their field trip to the museum. Once the students begin to get hooked on art, it is very easy to combine reading activities with art appreciation.

Any teacher, with or without formal art training, can put art to work in the classroom to stimulate the interest of pupils toward every subject or skill area, including reading. Teacher attitudes, interests, and beliefs that students can learn important reading skills through art appreciation are key factors in determining the success of art and reading activities.

Increasing Vocabulary While Studying Art

The visual image of something that can be described by a new word helps develop new vocabulary by association. While helping students to appreciate and better enjoy the works of artists, it is desirable to use the language of art. This is an exciting way to expand vocabularies and increase fluency in verbal expression as students describe paintings and their reactions to them. Learning and using new descriptive words while discussing and writing about art works can enlarge vocabularies as well as give students more pleasure when viewing works of art. Art books that provide an introduction to basic art terms are readily available at libraries and bookstores.

Some of the concepts and related vocabulary that students can learn while viewing works of art can include words that express how the painting makes them feel (gloomy, excited, perplexed, peaceful, sad, happy), words that denote the formal aspects of a painting (such as the use of line, repetition, perspective, distortion, space, mass, contrast, texture, color, shade, balance, composition), words that describe the medium and techniques employed (oils, watercolor, sketch, pastels, charcoal, wash), and words which refer to the subject of the painting or to the cultural and physical setting in which the painting was created.

The new vocabulary that will help students appreciate, enjoy, better interpret, and analyze art work can be introduced gradually. To help retain the new words, explain the new terms in reference to specific works of art that the students can see. Write the new terms on the board with brief explanatory phrases or sentences, and ask the students to explain the new terms in their own words or give synonyms for them. When discussing other pictures, the new words can be used repeatedly to reinforce the newly acquired words and concepts.

Individual students or the class as a whole can develop a dictionary of art words. New terms can be placed on a bulletin board with art reproductions that are illustrative. For example, when studying distortion, pictures by El Greco that show people with very elongated bodies can be studied and displayed on a bulletin board surrounding the word "distortion" and its definition. Or when studying the use of colors and artists' reasons for using different colors, reproductions of paintings by van Gogh, Rousseau, Picasso, Remington, and Chagall can be displayed along with relevant descriptive terms. Students can be helped to see that van Gogh often used brilliant oranges, reds, yellows, and blues when he was living in southern France where it was sunny and warm; Rousseau used shades of green to show the mysterious nature of his jungles; Remington used dusty oranges, browns, and yellows to indicate the dryness of the West; Chagall used pastels to create a feeling of fantasy; and Picasso used blues to reflect a moody feeling. Works of artists can be displayed and discussed to show how they often used colors differently throughout their lives as their interests, concerns, and moods changed.

To enlarge their vocabularies, students may be asked to describe and name the many shades of color in specific paintings, such as all the shades of blue in Picasso's "Guitar Player." They can discuss the reasons artists might have had for using different colors. Why did Toulouse-Lautrec often paint a woman with red hair? Why did Chagall paint a violin player with a green face in "The Green Violinist"? Students can look for uses of color in other pictures and discuss how color can create feelings of happiness, excitement, sadness, and fantasy. They can read poems about colors to see how colors can be described in words. Students can write stories about color and use different colors to encode their thoughts while they are using new terms to ensure their meaningful retention.

Students usually know what they like or dislike about a painting, but often they cannot easily or effectively tell why. If students are provided with words that will enable them to better express themselves, they will not only be enlarging their speaking and reading vocabularies, but they will be expanding their abilities to enjoy and appreciate the works of art around them by being better able to communicate their thoughts, feelings, and interpretations of art.

For review, the students can play charades, lotto, twenty questions, or Scrabble, using only art terms. They can write and read captions for paintings, using new descriptive terms. They can hypothesize as to the artists' selections of titles for their paintings. They can have small group contests to list all the things seen in complex, detailed paintings such as Chagall's "Paris through the Window" or Picasso's "Night Fishing at Antibes," or they can describe all the ways a painting makes them feel. Thus, students' understanding and reading vocabularies can be enlarged in a variety of ways while their eyes are being opened to the world of great art.

Developing Comprehension Skills through Art Appreciation

Art works and reading materials are both means of communication and they must be understood to be fully appreciated. Understanding or comprehension is not just a reading skill; it is a thinking skill, and when students are helped to better understand and interpret an artistic creation, they are being helped to further develop the thinking/comprehending abilities so necessary for effective reading.

To fully understand a work of art, one needs to attempt to grasp both the surface creation of the artist as well as the underlying feelings embodied in the created work. If a person looks at an artistic creation and merely ascertains that the artist has painted a girl lying on the grass looking at a house, as in "Christina's World" by Andrew Wyeth, the viewer has really just seen the painting on the surface and has missed the intended message that needs to be inferred. Understanding art involves "reading between the brush strokes" and understanding how artists feel as they create a work of art. Students need help in comprehending artistic creations on higher levels as they also need help in inferring messages in print. Helping students to "read" between and beyond the brush strokes of a painting can make them more aware of the need to seek meaning beyond the surface or literal meaning of printed words.

A student's enjoyment of a painting or a literary work is part intellectual and part emotional. Some impressionistic, surrealistic, and romantic paintings (such as those by Monet, Toulouse-Lautrec, Miro, Klee, Chagall, and Dali) appeal first to the emotions or imagination. Other, more realistic paintings (Harnett, Brueghel, Remington, and Stuart) appeal strongest to the intellect. Students often need to be encouraged to respond to art work emotionally as well as intellectually.

Some people are unable to fully enjoy art because of their mistaken beliefs that art is communication of something recognizable only to the learned and informed, and that everyone should get the same message from a work of art. Everyone can perceive something in an art work and react to it in some way, but individuals rarely react in the same way or get the same meaning. Art viewing usually arouses a variety of meanings and feelings which, although they can be shared, are personal and unique to each individual. It is important to help students feel free to differ in their thinking, interpretations, and opinions. Such divergent viewpoints and appreciations should be encouraged when reflecting on many literary works. Although we should not stipulate what students should feel about a painting, a great deal can be done to improve sensitivity to art. Students cannot react meaningfully to something they do not understand; and the more they learn about a painting, the artist, and the medium used, the deeper their understanding and appreciation will be.

Students can be helped to improve their literal comprehension skills as they study the surface meaning of a painting. For instance, when studying "Red Horses" by Marc, relevant questions can be asked concerning the artist's choice of color for the horses, the type of setting, time of day or movement of the horses. When looking at "Snowing" by Chagall, students could be asked to describe the clown's clothing, compare it to clothing worn by clowns today, discuss the different colors used in the painting, or identify and describe the musical instrument the clown is playing.

Inferential thinking skills can also be further developed when studying art because a work of art is not merely imitation like a photograph; it also reveals the artist's interpretation of the subject or theme. Just as authors use words which are symbols to carry their meanings, artists use symbols such as colors, shades, and forms to convey their feelings. Students must be helped to recognize the artist's interpretations, feelings, motivations, opinions, and possible prejudices and see how visual images can be used to convey many types of messages. If students do not understand the symbols used in art works, they will lose much of the intended meaning such as in Picasso's "Guernica" in which a bull represents the pride and courage of Spain, and the horse the agony of war.

Similarly, unintended meanings can be read into an art work to change the artist's original intent. For example, in "The Peaceable Kingdom" by Edward Hicks, a Quaker preacher, the animals, children, Indians, and William Penn illustrate Hicks' belief in peace on earth and goodwill toward men. His painting illustrates three verses from the eleventh chapter of Isaiah: "The wolf also shall dwell with the lamb, and the leopard shall lie down with the kid, and the calf and the young lion and the fatling together; and a little child shall lead them. And the cow and the bear shall feed; their young ones shall lie down together; and the lion shall eat straw like the ox." If students are unaware of this painting's historical and Biblical references, "The Peaceable Kingdom" will be only a curious collection of animals, children, and men. When viewing paintings, ask questions to start students thinking between and beyond the brush strokes so they will be alerted to "read" the message-carrying images. For instance, ask students why they think Dali often painted clocks with elongated, distorted faces.

Through studying art, students can be helped to develop a better understanding of the interaction between a creator's feelings and the techniques used. When a poet writes a poem, there is a constant interplay between feelings and words chosen. When an artist paints, there is constant interplay between the feelings of the artist and the materials used (brush, paints, canvas). Help students explore the reasons an artist may have used certain materials, colors, and techniques and discuss the artist's possible feelings while using them. For instance, why did van Gogh use heavy brush strokes or why did Seurat express himself through tiny dots of color? Could van Gogh have been feeling angry, frustrated, or filled with enthusiasm when he used heavy brush strokes? What could Seurat have been thinking about when painting those tiny dots of color?

Through the study of paintings, students can learn to look at an artistic or literary creation from its location in time and place. Artists and authors are products of the attitudes and customs of their cultures at the time in which they lived. Artists usually reflect some aspects of their contemporary culture in their works because they are a part of it. In addition, they often reveal their own personal feelings about their society. Sometimes it is easier for students to grasp this relationship in paintings than in literary works. Paintings by El Greco, Goya, and Velazquez have a message for us, whether we know Spanish or anything about the period in which they lived. The more we know of these artists and their worlds, the better we can understand their paintings. Some students might be able to readily identify with the works of Grandma Moses or Norman Rockwell, but might need more help in interpreting the works of Rembrandt or Goya in terms of their more distant historical and social background. Information concerning the cultural background of artists can be found in encyclopedia, art books, and biographical materials that are available in school and public libraries.

When surrounded by paintings, students can broaden their conceptual knowledge which will enable them to better visualize things read in print. Much can be learned from paintings about the historical times of the artists. From the walls of Egyptian tombs we can learn about the days of the reign of King Tut; from early paintings in caves in Spain, we can learn about the importance of the bison to early man; and from the paintings of Brueghel, we can learn much about the lives of ordinary people—the games they played, the food they ate, and how they celebrated. Life in early America can become more real to jet age students through studying paintings by Copley, Stuart, Remington, and the self-taught American Primitives, including Joseph Badger.

Carefully selected paintings can add a great deal to reading in the content areas, especially in social studies and science. All civilizations have their own art and, by studying it, we can learn more about how the people of a certain age or location lived, what clothes they wore, what food they ate, and what they did in their daily lives. Biographies and some of the fictionalized biographies of artists (such as *Lust for Life* about van Gogh, *The Agony and the Ecstasy* about Michelangelo, and *The Moon and Sixpence* about Gauguin) can give students an indication of how artists fit into and reflect their cultures. Letters and excerpts from diaries of artists, such as those found in *Letters of Great*

Artists, can give students insights into the money problems and financial affairs of artists. The way artists fit into the economic life of different cultures is an interesting aspect of economics, because their training, materials, and support are all expensive items. Sociology can also be enlivened by studying paintings which illustrate different levels and needs of society, such as some of the later paintings of Rembrandt, selected works by van Gogh and Goya, and the very descriptive works of Brueghel. Students might want to read and learn more about foreign cultures after looking at the works of foreign artists such as Orozco and Rivera from Mexico. Younger students could learn more about animals, flowers, and children of other times and lands by carefully studying selected prints.

While students are talking about art, they are refining their verbal skills, using their new vocabulary of art terms, and strengthening their minds and vocabulary to describe, analyze, interpret, and make personal judgments concerning paintings. All of these skills have a direct relationship to reading.

DIRECTED ART AND READING ACTIVITY

1. Introduction and Motivation

    Motivate students to want to observe and study a painting by briefly discussing the subject matter, such as clowns, dogs, children, or scenery. Write on the board an interest-arousing sentence such as, "How would you paint a watch to show how you feel about time?" (Dali's "The Persistence of Memory") "What do you think we could learn about games by studying a painting that is over 400 years old?" (Brueghel's "Children's Games")

    Give some anecdotal background about the artist such as remarks on van Gogh's temperament, Gauguin's move to Tahiti, or Picasso's varied artistic interests. Discuss opinions of the painting or arouse student's curiosity about the technique, such as, "Can you imagine how you would paint using only tiny dots of color as Seurat did?" "Why do you think van Gogh expressed himself with thick swirls of color?"

2. Initial Reaction Time

    Give students time to look at and discuss a projected color slide or reproduction of a painting. Ask them to discuss or write down their reactions to and feelings about the painting.

3. Introduction of New Vocabulary and Concepts

Depending on the age and developmental level of the students, discuss criteria that might be helpful in studying the painting: color, mood, technique, symbolism, or choice of subject matter. Write new terms on the board and have students explain them in their own words. Discuss the cultural background of the artist including (when relevant) national, ethnic, philosophical, and religious influences on the artist. Show slides or color reproductions of other paintings by the same artist or paintings by other artists dealing with the same subject.

4. Directed Viewing

Give students time to study the painting again in light of the new knowledge. Give them something specific on which to focus: use of colors, perspective, representation of subject matter, artist's interpretations and/or feelings. The students can discuss or write their reactions.

5. Follow-Up Activities

Activities can include a debate or panel discussion reflecting different views of the painting; student written and produced plays about the artist's life or creation of a specific painting; student written poems about the painting, artist, or subject of the painting; location of other poems that would exemplify the picture; student written descriptive riddles dealing with some aspect of the painting; reports on the artist and interpretations of the painting.

References

Blake, W. Tygre, tygre, burning bright. In R. Abcarian (Ed.), *Words in flight*. Belmont, California: Wadsworth, 1972.

Bookbinder, J. Art and reading. *Language Arts*, 1976, *52*, 783-785.

Chambers, D. Children's literature and the allied arts. *Elementary English*, 1971, *48*, 622-627.

Chase, A.E. *Famous paintings: An introduction to art*. New York: Platt & Munk, 1962.

Dewey, J. *Art as experience*. New York: Putnam, 1934.

Eliot, A. *Three hundred years of american painting*. Time, 1975.

Erickson, R., & Thomas, E.L. Art class book collection promotes better reading. *Journal of Reading*, 1968, *11*, 333-336.

Friedenthal, R. *Letters of great artists*. New York: Random House, 1963.

Garcia, L.B. Art history for grade two. *School Arts*, 1966, *66*, 10-12.

Glasser, W., & Day, M. Every classroom's a gallery. *School Arts*, 1973, *72*, 22-23.

Green, F. Art helps us read. *Art and Activities*, 1965, *57*, 17.

Groff, P. Critics corner—art and reading: Is there a relationship? *Reading World*, May 1978, 345.

Huck, C., & Kuhn, D. *Children's literature in the elementary school.* New York: Holt, Rinehart & Winston, 1968.

Joseph, M.F. Children, art, and literature. *School Arts,* November 1969, 28-29.

Kirk, Ada. Art a vehicle for English. *Texas Outlook,* December 1967, 22-23.

Kohn, Jackie. Art spark. *Arts and Activities,* 1974, *76,* 30-32.

Labrecque, C. Art in the classroom: Pictures motivate creative writing. *Teacher,* 1968, *85,* 91.

Locke, O. Another way of seeing. *School Arts,* June 1974, 20-21.

Maugham, W.S. *The moon and sixpence.* New York: Modern Library, 1919.

McLuhan, M. *Understanding media.* New York: McGraw-Hill, 1974.

O'Neill, M. *Hailstones and halibut bones.* Garden City, New York: Doubleday, 1961.

Poe, E.A. *The pit and the pendulum.* Garden City, New York: Complete Stories Press, 1966.

Raboff, E. *Art for children.* Garden City, New York: Doubleday, 1969.

Reimer, B. Teaching aesthetic perception. *Education Forum,* 1966, *30,* 349-356.

Remington, F. *Frederic Remington and our west.* New York: Dial Press, 1960.

Rios, J.F. Research in art in the teaching of reading. *American Childhood Journal,* 1955, *40,* 13-15.

Rossetti, C. What is pink? In L. Boga and W. Smith (Eds.), *The golden journey: Poems for young people.* Chicago: Reilly & Lee, 1965.

Schmidt, J. The process of appreciation. *Art Education,* 1973, *26,* 12-13.

Stone, I. *The agony and the ecstasy.* Garden City, New York: Doubleday, 1961.

Stone, I. *Lust for life.* New York: Pocket Books, 1963.

Wilbur, R. Museum piece. In R. Abcarian (Ed.), *Words in flight.* Belmont, California: Wadsworth, 1972.

Reading, Creative Writing, and the Literary Arts

Chants, Charts, and 'Chievement

Robert A. McCracken
Western Washington University
Marlene J. McCracken
Surrey School District No. 36
Surrey, British Columbia

Children learn language by experience. The teacher should provide the experience, present ideas, and use language to hold ideas together. The teacher presents the totality of language. Children then analyze language and work to learn it. The teacher teaches and the children practice using the language until it is learned.

We know of no better way for children to learn language than to hear language, to see the language they hear come into print, and then to work with the bits of language. Teaching time is less than practice time—a ratio of perhaps one hour of teaching for each ten to twenty hours of practice. Teaching is usually to large groups or the total class; practice is usually in very small groups or individually. The heart of any individualized program is in allowing children to practice individually in ways that allow them to learn. This means teaching that appeals to all senses; and it means providing many ways to practice. Each child builds an individual learning program and practices.

Chanting and song are two of the easiest ways to teach children some complete units of meaningful language. Chantable material is usually poetry. It will have strong rhythm, an easily discernible structure and, perhaps, rhyme; it will make sense and yet have a bit of mystery to challenge children to make sense. Mother Goose rhymes are a good example. They have rhythm, structure, rhyme, and suggest more than literal meaning or that much of the story has been omitted. "Little Boy Blue" suggests something more than an indolent boy; "Mary, Mary

Quite Contrary" suggests something more than a naughty girl. It may be that mystery and lack of literal meaning help rhymes endure.

There are two basic ways children work individually with written language to practice and learn. 1) They read. Most commonly, this is silent reading. Sustained silent reading is one form we advocate, but it is not the purpose of this paper to discuss silent reading (McCracken & McCracken, 1972). 2) Children write. They read to others what they have written and they read what classmates have written, but the important part of writing is the working with bits and pieces of language, the taking apart of an idea into its pieces in order to record it.

To write and to learn to write, children need ideas, words to express the ideas, the ability to spell (McCracken & McCracken, 1978), and structures upon which to impose their ideas. This paper is concerned primarily with some of the structures children may use to express ideas. It is vital that oral work precede writing attempts—oral work to develop the ideas and vocabulary needed. Oral work also develops structures because it is the structure that enables children to put ideas on paper, and it is through structures that are practiced and repracticed that drill with language is provided (McCracken & McCracken, 1978). Most children's perception of structures is intuitive. We chant a poem, a chant, a song lyric, or we sing. We repeat a song or chant so often that the structure becomes a part of the child's repertoire.

For example, over a period of one to two weeks we sing and dance "The Farmer in the Dell" until every child knows it by heart; we present it visually on the chalkboard, on a chart, on sentence strips, on word cards, and in book form. In small groups and individually, the children work with the sentence strips and the word cards to put the song into its proper sequence. In doing so they chant or sing over and over again as a natural response to their ordering activities.

During the school year, we have children practice using the structure of "The Farmer in the Dell" as a vehicle to express ideas developed in discussion or from books. The teacher and the class write many takeoffs as a group, and then children develop individual takeoffs. Frequently, takeoffs are created in book form and on charts. The creators teach their lyrics to the class as they all sing. The following are primary grade takeoffs:

> The witch is in the air.
> The witch is in the air.
> Boo, boo, she's scaring you.
> The witch is in the air.

The goblin's out tonight.
The goblin's out tonight.
Don't be scared; he won't eat you.
The goblin's out tonight.

Santa's in his sleigh.
Santa's in his sleigh.
Oh, my, he's flying high.
Santa's in his sleigh.

The lake is frozen hard.
The lake is frozen hard.
Skate, skate, for goodness sake.
The lake is frozen hard.

Be my valentine.
Be my valentine.
Let's be friends forevermore.
Be my valentine.

Pierre said, "I don't care!"
Pierre said, "I don't care!"
So the lion ate Pierre.
Pierre said, "I don't care!"

The wolf ate grand-ma-ma.
The wolf ate grand-ma-ma.
Oh, my, she's going to die.
The wolf ate grand-ma-ma.

The wolf ate Red Riding Hood.
The wolf ate Red Riding Hood.
Oh, my, she's going to die.
The wolf ate Red Riding Hood.

The woodman chopped them out.
The woodman chopped them out.
Oh, what a gooey mess!
The woodman chopped them out.

Each of these verses may be illustrated line by line and put on a chart for the whole class to use. The illustrations can be made large to form a chart song of several pages; or they can be small to make up an unbound book whose pages the children can sort and put in order.

This kind of song is particularly good in primary grades because there is so much repetition. The teacher does not have too much to teach before the children can begin writing and practicing. Most children can copy from the chart or chalkboard without particular attention from the teacher. However, we find that some children need the chance to copy on a chalkboard before they work with paper and pencil. It seems easier to teach children how to write by using chalk than by using a pencil. For some children, we provide sentence strips of each line so they can copy directly underneath onto the chalkboard. Individual chalkboards, unlined, measuring 12" x 18" are available from World Research Company. The teacher is thus able to work with those few children who need special help in writing while most of the children work independently.

We use jump rope jingles. We put these on charts, on sentence strips, and on individual cards.

> I woke up in the morning,
> I looked upon the wall.
> The cooties and the bedbugs
> Were having a game of ball.
>
> The score was ten to nothing.
> The cooties were ahead
> The bedbugs hit a home run,
> And knocked me out of bed.
>
> How many runs did they score?
> Twenty, thirty, maybe more.
> One, two, three, four....

A child might use this structure to write an episode from *Charlotte's Web.*

> Wilbur woke up one morning.
> And he began to wail.
> The rain was pouring down outside,
> When Lurvey brought his pail.
>
> Templeton began to eat,
> Wilbur sobbed and sobbed.
> He felt so very awful,
> He didn't care if he was robbed.
>
> How many scraps did Templeton eat?
> One, two, three, four....

McCracken and McCracken

Using the structure of "Sing a Song of Sixpence," we adapted to it the lyrics of McDonald's "Big Mac" advertising jingle, with the following results:

> Sing a song of Big Mac,
> Sesame bun,
> Two all-beef patties,
> Very well done.
> Onions, pickles, lettuce,
> Cheese and special sauces.
> Please don't burp and please don't slurp,
> Or Mother will be cross!

The pizza lovers composed:

> Sing a song of pizza,
> Mozzarella cheese.
> Put on lots of bacon,
> Some anchovies, please.
> When the pizza is baked,
> We all begin to eat. Isn't that a gooey dish
> To carry down the street!

We have read orally to a class, *Magic in the Mist* by Margaret Mary Kimmel (Kimmel, 1975) and then worked with one of the book's main ideas, Thomas' inability to make a proper incantation. We have added "Chanting Cant" to the presentation and chanted orally:

> Lots of people don't believe in
> Wizards and the like.
> Lots of people can't conceive of
> Magic in the night.

> Lots of people ne'er receive a
> Message from a genie,
> But lots of people never learn
> To chant their chants just right.

> So if you ever want to be
> A witch, a sorcerer, or such,
> You'll have to practice incanting chants
> Until you've got the touch.

Then we have written all sorts of chants and practiced incantations. The first step in writing a chant is brainstorming to get a list of words. A list is the simplest form of writing. The list itself provides unity because lists are things that go together. We can list all the ice cream flavors we know, all the spices used in cooking, or all the animals of the world. We can list sports, TV shows, and TV characters. Putting them together is very simple, as long as the last syllable of each line is accented. For example:

CHANT FOR GOOD EATING

Bay leaf, parsley, tarragon, dill.
Cayenne pepper, peppercorn mill.
Thyme, ginger root, cinnamon, salt.
Sesame, poppyseed, sage, and malt.

Or we brainstorm for all the things that hands can do or that children like to do (or don't like to do). Following is a partial list that has been recorded on the chalkboard:

tap	wave	squeeze	fold	write	sew
hold	wiggle	freeze	scratch	dial	stitch
rap	mold	signal	scrape	point	splash
pinch	rub	scribble	strap	paint	splice
type	sign	snap	clap	wiggle	scold

We print each word from the list on a large card and write several chants in the pocket chart, chanting each chant orally. The children compose chants that they particularly like. For example, we may group the words by rhyme:

Tap, snap, clap, rap.
Hold, mold, fold, scold.
Hands! Hands! Hands!

We may group by meaning:

Color, scribble, write, type.
Embroider, knit, stitch, sew.
Hands! Hands! Hands!

We may group alliteratively:

Scribble, squeeze, scratch, scrape.
Point, paint, pinch, pull.
Hands! Hands! Hands!

We may combine all six lines, chanting Hands! Hands! Hands! only once. We may add an inflectional ending to change the rhyme of the chant. In so doing, we teach or review the ways to add inflectional *ing*:

Coloring, scribbling, writing, typing.
Embroidering, knitting, stitching, sewing.
Hands! Hands! Hands!

We may use the word "hands" in several ways:

Scribbling hands
Scratching hands
Scraping hands
Squeezing hands

Hands scribbling
Hands scratching
Hands scraping
Hands squeezing

Hands scribble and scratch
Hands scrape and squeeze

Scribbling, scratching hands
Squeezing, scraping hands

By putting together several groupings, or by making the praises into complete sentences, we extend the chants as follows:

I use my hands to write and type,
　　　　　　　to scratch and scrape,
　　　　　　　to paint and point.

I clap my hands to show what I like.

I rap with my hands on my neighbor's door.

I fold my hands to say a prayer.

I rub my hands to get them warm.

Rap, tap, write, type,
snap, clap, scratch, scrape.

Point, paint, hold, fold,
wiggle, wave, stitch and sew.

H - A - N - D - S—HANDS!

We can sing using "The Farmer in the Dell":

Write, write, write.
Write, write, write.
With my hands I can write.
Write, write, write.

Clap, clap, clap.
Clap, clap, clap.
Clap my hands to show what I like.
Clap, clap, clap.

Tap, rap, write.
Tap, rap, write.
I really use my hands,
Tap, rap, write.

H - A - N - D - S
H - A - N - D - S
Wiggle, wave, stitch and sew
H - A - N - D - S.

We can "Sing a Song of Clapping Hands":

Sing a song of clapping hands
at the music show.
Every time they play a song
I clap and clap and clap.
When the show is over
I clap my hands some more.
If it's been a really great show,
My hands are really sore.

We use the song, "There'll Be a Hot Time in the Old Town Tonight" because it is one of the easiest structures to use:

One dark night when we were all in bed,
Old Mrs. Leary left a lantern in the shed.
When the cow kicked it over
She winked her eye and said,
"There'll be a hot time
In the old town tonight."

This easily works into:

Write, write, write,
I use my hands to write.
Type, type, type,
I use my hands to type.

Paint, paint, paint,
I use my hands to paint.
I'll use my left hand
And my right hand, today.

A year's use of chants and charts results in language achievement.

References

Fowke, E. *Ring around the moon.* Toronto, Ontario: McClelland & Stewart, 1977.

Fowke, E. *Sally go 'round the sun.* Toronto, Ontario: McClelland & Stewart, 1969.

Kimmel, M.M. *Magic in the mist.* New York: Atheneum, 1975.

McCracken, M.J., & McCracken, R.A. *Reading, writing and language.* Winnipeg, Manitoba: Peguis, 1979.

McCracken, M.J., & McCracken, R.A. Spelling booklet. University of North Dakota, Center for Teaching and Learning, 1978.

McCracken, R.A. Do we want real readers? *Journal of Reading,* 1969, *12,* 446-448.

McCracken, R.A. Initiating sustained silent reading. *Journal of Reading,* 1971, *14,* 521-524.

McCracken, R.A., & McCracken, M.J. *Reading is only the tiger's tail.* San Rafael, California: Leswing, 1972.

Milne, A.A. *Now we are six.* New York: E.P. Dutton, 1937.

Milne, A.A. *When we were very young.* New York: E.P. Dutton, 1938.

Silverstein, S. *Where the sidewalk ends.* New York: Harper & Row, 1974.

Skolnick, P.L. *Jump rope!* New York: Workman, 1974.

Worstell, E.V. *Jump the rope jingles.* New York: Macmillan, 1961.

World Research Company, 307 S. Beckham Street, Tyler, Texas 75701. (Source of good quality, inexpensive, individual chalkboards.)

Conversations with Poet Jose Garcia Villa
on Teaching Poetry to Children

John E. Cowen
Teaneck, New Jersey, Public Schools

Jose Garcia Villa, National Artist of the Philippines, has lived in the United States for the past forty years, and has been the recipient of the American Academy of Arts and Letters Award. His first three volumes of poetry (Villa 1942, 1949, 1958) have won him the high esteem of distinguished fellow poets and critics, among them Dame Edith Sitwell, Mark Van Doren, Marianne Moore, and e.e. cummings (Villa 1979).

For two decades, Villa has shared his views on poetic theory and process with students attending his poetry workshops offered at the New School for Social Research and at his Greenwich Village apartment. Recently, he discussed with me his views on the art of reading and writing poetry for children. In this article, it is my intention to share these conversations in which Villa's theories of poetics are discussed. As a result we, as teachers, may become more sensitized to the poetic process and, in this instance, to a particular poet's point of view.

Once teachers have a feel for poetry and have some notion about the poetic process, they will refrain from asking questions that take children outside of the poem. They will focus on questions that ask how and why, while noting sound correlations, tensions of language, rhythms of language, tone, mood, and magic evoked by the poem.

Teachers need to help children distinguish between *what* literature means and *how* literature means, particularly if they intend to develop children's real appreciation of the various literary genres. Children must learn to distinguish between knowing *what* the poem is saying and *how* it is saying it. And if teachers intend to improve children's expressive language, they must provide opportunities for students to present their ideas, both orally and in writing. Furthermore, if children are truly going to understand the medium of poetry, they should learn how to go about writing poetry the way a capable poet does. Therefore, children must not be burdened with the pedantic "whatness" of poetry but must find the magic in poetry.

Although Villa has never consciously written poems for children, a number of his poems have appeared in anthologies for young readers (appropriate for ten to seventeen year olds) including *Speaking for Ourselves* (Faderman, Bradshaw, 1968); *New Voices* (Clive, Conlon et al., 1978); and *Adventures in American Literature* (Hodgins et al., 1980).

Poetry for Younger Children

Perhaps since Villa has always placed the magicality of language before subject matter and meaning, many of his poems delight children. I recently asked Villa why children enjoy his poems if he never consciously writes for children. "Perhaps it's because I just play with language as children play with words," was his response. "There's a child in me that comes out. I always believed that when you're writing poems, you can't be just your actuality, but the child must remain in you. The sense of imaginative play comes out."

I reminded Villa that critics often compare his work to William Blake's because of his childlike visionary quality. "But William Blake was not really childlike; I am more childlike than he," Villa charged. "Blake didn't really play in the sense of play. He just spoke like a child, in a child's language in his *Songs of Innocence*. When I write, I play like a kitten plays with a ball of yarn. I push language around and play with it, the way a kitten plays."

Sitwell gives credence to Villa's assertion in her introduction to his *Selected Poems and New*, stating: "These poems grow, *often from the language*, which is the matrix. As Mallarme said, a poem is 'written not with ideas, but with words.' "

Poets Villa Recommends for Children

Villa has always recommended that students attending his poetry workshops read the good poets—John Donne, Gerald Manley Hopkins, e.e. cummings, Dylan Thomas, Wilfred Owen, Emily

Dickinson, Elinor Wylie, and Marianne Moore—especially if they intend to become serious poets (Williams, 1960).

"What poets would you recommend children to read?" I asked him. The poets that came immediately to mind included Emily Dickinson, Robert Frost, e.e. cummings, Nathalia Crane, Lewis Carroll, Edward Lear (Williams, 1960) "and don't forget the nursery rhymes for the very young child," he reminded.

"Emily Dickinson's, *Good Morning, Midnight*, would appeal to a child; and *You Come, Too*, by Robert Frost has a childlike quality," Villa said. "Some of Cummings' poems can certainly be enjoyed by children, just for their sound values alone, like 'anyone lived in a pretty how town/ (with up so floating many bells down)/ spring summer autumn winter/ he sang his didn't he danced his did,'...and so on." Villa continued, "Edward Lear's limericks would appeal to children because they depend on rhyme, and Lewis Carroll played with language and was fanciful; children can learn from him. Children may even find poetry in Gertrude Stein's *The World is Round* (Stein, 1939) which is technically not a poem; it was written in prose but, at the same time, it has that essential playfulness of poetry in it and children would appreciate it." (The famous line "...a rose is a rose is a rose" is often quoted from this work.)

Contrary to widespread practice in American schools, Villa is not enamored of the Haiku for children because it does not depend on rhyme, and he does not think children should write by counting syllables, which he believes is a method that goes contrary to the child.

Villa's Philosophy Stated in Bravo

On the back cover of the first issue of *Bravo*, a poetry magazine edited by Jose Garcia Villa (December 1980), the poet succinctly states his philosophy of poetry. *Bravo* believes that:

1. Poetry must have formal excellence.
2. Poetry must be lyrical.
3. Poetry is *not* prose.

Villa's distinction here should indicate that most of the poetry written today is simply prose chopped into short lines, masquerading as poetry. Furthermore, in bold type, almost as a personal challenge to contemporary poetry and editors, Villa declares: **"Diamonds Are In...Beans Are Out!"** By *beans*, Villa means works that entail no effort—facile, instant, and easy; by *diamonds*, he means that hard won, inviolable, diamondlike quality of the true poem.

Yet, Villa holds a somewhat less demanding view when speaking about young children's poetry. "Just allow the child's imagination and poetic sense to run free. I'd just read a great deal to children and see how they enjoy the poems. For children's poetry, their imaginations should enflame the words." Villa believes in nourishing spontaneity in children. "Encourage the child to observe and speak more," he advises. "When children speak, there is already a poetic quality evident because of their innocence. It comes out sweet and has a surprising quality," Villa reminds us. And when children are given the opportunity to write down their observations, he contends, "Children can hear the rhythm of language. They'll be aware of the quality of the magic in the line. They're economical; they wouldn't write long poems as many adult poets do."

As you read, listen to the sweet and surprising quality of the next two poems composed by children (ages seven and five respectively) which appeared in *Miracles*, a wonderful collection of poems by children of the English speaking world (Richard Lewis, 1966). The first poem, written by Tomas Santos, also appeared in Villa's *Doveglion Anthology of Philippine Poetry* (1965).

A Wish

I want to climb the santol tree
That grows beside my bedroom window
And get a santol fruit.
I want to climb the tree at night
And get the moon the branches hide.
Then I shall go to bed, my pockets full,
One with the fruit, the other with the moon.

This second lyrical poem was composed by Etain Mary Clarke (from Ireland), a pure poem sprung from her sweet innocence:

The Field of the Mice and the Marigold

The wind of the marigold,
The flies of the American Bird,
The shamrocks of the stones,
The Lord of the Fieldmice,
The marigold of the shamrocks,
The mice of the round-a-gold.
The tractors of the storm
How the wind blows
The wolves howl,
While the moon moves
Along the sky.

The wind blows people's hats off
And blows people's dresses up.
The Lord Mayor of the Dreams,
The mari-of-the-golds,
The Lord Mayor of the Golds.

When Dylan Thomas was asked which poets or kinds of poetry he was first moved and influenced by, he replied:

> The first poems I knew were nursery rhymes, and before I could read them for myself I had come to love just the words of them, the words alone. What the words stood for, symbolized, or meant, was of very secondary importance; what mattered was the *sound* of them as I heard them for the first time on the lips of the remote and incomprehensible grown-ups who seemed, for some reason, to be living in my world. . . .I did not care what the words said, overmuch, nor what happened to Jack and Jill and the Mother Goose rest of them; I cared for the *shapes of sound* that *their names* and *the words* describing their *actions* made in my ears; I cared for the colours the words cast on my eyes." (Sinclair, 1975)

I sometimes think that our contemporary poets have been deprived of this great opportunity to experience nursery rhymes, since they are so quick to abandon rhyme in their own work. This disinterest in rhyme seems to have crept into the classroom as well. In the December 12, 1973 *New York Times Book Review* of Kenneth Koch's *Wishes, Lies, and Dreams* (1970), a teacher's handbook on teaching children to write poetry, John Gardner points out that Koch discourages the use of rhyme, for he believes that rhyme tends to limit imagination and honest feeling. As for the child's question, "What shall I write?" Gardner reports that Koch worked out a set of simple, essentially formal *ideas* to assist the child in writing the poem. One is, "Begin every line with, 'I wish. . .' or 'I dreamt. . .'."

Villa's response to such an approach to teaching writing to children is that it would not allow children to develop their own minds. He suggests, "Just tell children to write about anything, and just let them write. I wouldn't give them an assigned subject or an assigned line. When a child makes an observation such as, 'Look, there's a plaid rainbow there in the sky,' encourage the child to write that line down. With proper encouragement, reading, guidance, and opportunity to write, the child will learn to build from such a naturally produced first line. That is how all good poets begin."

Putting this issue aside, I should add that Koch's *Wishes, Lies, and Dreams* can still be a useful text for teachers. Koch is at his best when he says:

> Sometimes a student would be stuck, unable to start his poem. I would give him a few ideas, while trying *not* to give him *actual lines or words*—"Well, how do musical instruments sound? Why don't you write about those?" Or, "What do

you hear when you're on a boat?" Sometimes students would get stuck in the middle of a poem, and I would do the same sort of thing. Sometimes I would be called over to approve what had been written so far, to see if it was OK. I often made such comments as, "That's good, but write some more," or "Yes, the first three lines in particular are terrific—what about some more like that?" Or, "I think maybe it's finished. What about another poem on the other side."

Once I shared with Villa two lines produced by my four-year-old daughter, Juliet: "I went out with a Siamese/and the Siamese began to sneeze." He remarked, "That is definitely poetry. You see," he continued, "children don't think of rhyme as rhyme, but they think of it as chiming; the chiming of sounds. Children *hear* much more than adult poets. Adult poets, today, don't hear at all. They are only making some kind of semantic sense. Let children hear the rhythm and let them chime, and that is really the poetic process. My aphorism," Villa added, " 'Love, is, much, ling, ling,/Very, much, ling, ling!' (Villa, 1979) depends on sound; at the same time it *means*. Love is like the ringing of a bell. That is what I mean by 'ling, ling!' Love tinkles so brightly."

Russian poet/critic Kornei Chukovsky is reported to have written that poems for small children "...must be graphic, for children think in images and there must be a rapid shift of imagery" (Smith, 1972). To this point, Villa argues, "Children don't think in images. They think in chimes or rhymes. Wherever chime or rhyme comes in, *that* is what creates the image. It is the rhyme that creates the image—not the image that creates the rhyme, and the rhyming creates the music and the rhythm in that order. The image, therefore, should be the *result* of language."

Poetic Techniques of Older Students

Villa believes that older children can begin seeing that form and technique are good for poetry and that as these students continue to mature, they should be exposed to more technical matters of poetry, experiencing, imitating, and solving the problems of craft the way a serious and more mature poet would.

As Dylan Thomas matured as a student, shortly before entering the eighth grade, he recalls, "I wrote endless imitations, though I never thought them to be imitations but, rather, wonderfully original things, like eggs laid by tigers. They were imitations of anything I happened to be reading at the time." In a short time, Thomas would be able to say, "What I like to do is treat words as a craftsman does his wood or stone or what-have-you, to hew, carve, mold, coil, polish, and plane them into patterns, sequences, sculptures, fugues of sound expressing some lyrical impulse, some spiritual doubt or conviction, some dimly-realized truth I must try to reach and realize" (Sinclair, 1975). Villa greatly respects Thomas's poetry, and would concur with the poet's observation regarding technique.

Villa's approach to poetry, simply stated, stresses the magic to be found in poetry rather than its meaning which is what most educational programs and texts emphasize. Only after the older student, or budding poet, considers the magical elements inherent in such techniques as the importance of the vivid first line; the musicality, tension, and movement of language; the intricasies of versification; the riches of metaphor; the necessity of economy; the element of surprise; and the implosive drama of the last line, will the neophyte begin to understand the power and magnificence of poetry. The prose meaning of the poem, therefore, is subsidiary—just as the poet discovers meaning through the writing of the poem, so will the reader discover "how the poem means."

Canadian poet, Margaret Atwood, echoes Villa's sentiments, stating:

> My poems usually begin with words or phrases which appeal more because of their sound than their meaning, and the movement and phrasing of a poem are very important to me...[therefore] it does annoy me when students, prompted by the approach of their teacher, ask, "What is the poet trying to say?" It implies that the poet is some kind of cripple who can't quite "say" what he "means" and has to resort to a lot of round-the-mulberry-bush, thereby putting the student to a great deal of trouble extracting the "meaning" like a prize out of a box of Cracker Jacks. (*New York Time Book Review*, May 21, 1978)

Villa's lyrical and exquisitely crafted poem, "First, a Poem Must Be Magical" (Villa, 1942), can serve as the basis for discussing his techniques of poetry. Although the poet did not set out to achieve this end, he does so, gracefully and economically. As you shall see, this beautiful poem leads to a unique definition of what a poem should be:

> First, a poem must be magical,
> Then musical as a seagull.
> It must be a brightness moving
> And hold secret a bird's flowering.
> It must be slender as a bell,
> And it must hold fire as well.
> It must have the wisdom of bows
> And it must kneel like a rose.
> It must be able to hear
> The luminance of dove and deer.
> It must be able to hide
> What it seeks, like a bride.
> And over all, I would like to hover
> God, smiling from the poem's cover.

In a taped interview, Villa provided me with an explication of this poem. Of the first two lines,

"First, a poem must be magical
Then musical as a sea gull."

Villa said, "These lines mean exactly what they say: That a poem must have magic, and it must be musical."

I asked the poet, "What meaning would you ascribe to the next lines?"

"It must be a brightness moving
And hold secret a bird's flowering."

Villa explained, "There are some brightnesses which are stationary and static, but a poem, like a bird, must fly. This is the difference between prose and poetry. Prose is flatfooted and stationary; poety soars, flies like a bird. The stationary bird, when first seen, appears like a rosebud. When it begins to fly, it opens up and spreads its wings and blooms like a flower."

I asked him to explain the images in the fifth and sixth lines,

"It must be slender as a bell
And it must hold fire as well."

To these lines, Villa responded, "A poem is economical; it's slender as a bell, it has no adipose tissue; it's lean and clean. Poorly written poems should, of necessity, go on a diet, to rid themselves of excess verbiage and adjectives. And by 'fire' in the next line, I simply mean that a poem must have a spirit."

"I have always found the next lines difficult to comprehend," I confessed:

"It must have the wisdom of bows
And it must kneel like a rose."

"You must remember," Villa said, "some lines and some poems cannot be explained. But let me try. I am speaking of the archer's bow. A good bow is one that knows when to shoot, and one that directs the arrow to its mark. Just as a good poem, it never goes astray. To 'kneel like a rose' is a metaphor for humility. All fine people are humble and a poem should also be humble, however beautiful it is."

For the seventh and eighth lines,

"It must be able to hear
The luminance of dove and deer."

"There's a good man behind every fine poem. A good poet is usually a good person. 'Luminance' naturally means brightness. When I see a good face, it's a good face and I respond. When I see a bad face, it is the face full of crime, even though he doesn't proclaim his crime. His face proclaims it out loud."

"In other words," I asked, "the poet knows things instinctively?"

"Yes, naturally," Villa answered.

And for the meaning of the next couplet, I prodded Villa to discuss,

"It must be able to hide
What it seeks, like a bride."

Villa, without hesitation, began, "A poem must *not explicitly* state meaning. The reader is supposed to sense it out, feel it. The language itself doesn't tell you, but the substructure behind that language is the real meaning. It is not explicit and declarative. That's why when I say, 'It must have the wisdom of bows,' you must guess at what I mean, and children love to guess at meaning. That's why they love riddles. I used to love riddles as a child."

The final couplet of this rather unorthodox sonnet,

"And over all I would like to hover
God, smiling from the poem's cover."

is possibly one of the most beautiful ever written. "The last line has a masterfully dramatic effect. At the same time, this couplet is, to me, the most mystifying one in the poem," I commented.

Villa nodded and offered this explanation: "When you see a blessed creature, God shines and hovers over that saintly creature. The poem itself creates a God-hood, and the poem radiates Godness. At the same time, God is hovering over it, acknowledging the Godness radiating from the poem, itself, which embodies the spirituality existing in a poem and, at the same time, radiates it to others."

Indeed, there is a Godness to this poem; and there is a God-hood within this poet. Poet Richard Eberhardt understood this, too, evidenced in a review of Villa's work in which he states:

> A pure, startling, and resounding body of poetry, informed with so much legerity and fire, remarkably consistent in its devotion to spiritual reality. The subject matter is formidable, the author a God-driven poet. He arrives at peaks without showing the strenuous effort of climbing; the personal is lost in a blaze of linguistic glories. . . .(Villa, 1958)

The poet concludes that reading poetry might be compared to enjoying riddles, and that children enjoy solving riddles. Since poetry is neither explicit nor declarative, children must be taught through sheer joy to sense out and feel the meaning. Is there not much of this that goes on when we are "sensing" or drawing conclusions, or making an inference? Perhaps we should become more concerned about providing children with joyous language experiences that will enable them to better understand poetry. Thus, we may begin to teach our children how to cope with poetry, not in a frustrating search for exact meaning but, rather, in a quest to understand linguistic glories.

References

Koch, K. *Wishes, lies, and dreams.* New York: Vintage, 1970.

Lewis, R. *Miracles.* New York: Bantam Books, 1977.

Sinclair, A. *Dylan Thomas, no man more magical.* New York: Holt, Rinehart & Winston, 1975.

Smith, W.J. *The streaks of the tulip.* New York: Delacorte Press/Seymore Lawrence, 1972.

Stein, G. *The world is round.* New York: W.R. Scott, 1939.

Villa, J.G. *Appassionata, poems in praise of love.* New York: King & Cowen, 1979.

Villa, J.G. Be beautiful, noble, like the antique ant. In W. Hodgins et al. (Eds.), *Adventures in American literature.* New York: Harcourt Brace Jovanovich, 1980.

Villa, J.G. (Ed.). *Bravo.* New York: Bravo Editions, 1980.

Villa, J.G. (Ed.). *Doveglion anthology of Philippine poetry.* Manila, Philippines: Caliraya Foundation, 1965.

Villa, J.G. First, a poem must be magical. In J. Cline et al. (Eds.), *New Voices 4.* Lexington, Massachusetts: Ginn, 1978.

Villa, J.G. *Have come, am here.* New York: Viking Press, 1942.

Villa, J.G. Inviting a tiger. In L. Faderman & B. Bradshaw (Eds.), *Speaking for ourselves.* Glenview, Illinois: Scott, Foresman, 1968.

Villa, J.G. *Selected poems and new.* New York: McDowell, Obolensky, 1958.

Villa, J.G. *Volume two.* New York: New Directions, 1949.

Williams, O. (Ed.). *Immortal poems of the English language.* New York: Washington Square Press, 1960.

Children's Literature:
An Enhancement in Language Development

Sally A. Chant
Penn State University, Capitol Campus

Introduction

Young children are in a period of tremendous language and concept development. Firsthand and vicarious experiences add to this rapid development. Children's literature must not be overlooked as a benefit in this area. Recommendations of literary materials and suggestions for their use by preschool and primary teachers are offered in this discussion.

A lifelong love affair with books is one gift every child should be given. The three good fairies in *Sleeping Beauty* gave wondrous gifts to the little princess, to be sure, but none were so wondrous as those supplied by words. Words and pictures open worlds. Between the covers of each new book, a new experience is waiting. Watch the children's eyes open wide with excitement as they turn the front cover to reveal glorious colors and black print on crisp white pages. Here tugboats and elephants, magical dragons and castles, spring to life! Young children can't wait to identify the mysterious black shapes that turn into meaningful concepts as they learn to read.

Teachers have gifts to give: enjoyment, entertainment, creativity, understanding of self, and the ability to reason. Those gifts begin in the classroom with children's literature. When teachers read to children, they can immediately turn the experience into an active one. Children can be encouraged to ask questions; to relate incidents that have happened to them which parallel those in the book; to discuss what is happening and try to decide what the outcome of the book might be. Teachers have the opportunity, too, to stop and discuss an unfamiliar word. By occasionally using a child's beginning dictionary with bright pictures, the children see a pattern emerge which will be of utmost value to them through school and beyond. A new word appears. Stop! Look it up in the dictionary. Continue reading. Beginning vocabularies are expanded effortlessly and continuously as a natural part of the reading process. On other occasions, the mere discussion of a word's meaning will be sufficient.

Books, once completed, are not "over and done with." Children read and reread dearly-loved books. Completed books can provide a myriad of opportunities for continued learning in the classroom. They can be turned into paintings, puppet shows, dramatic plays, or music. They serve in this way to spark latent creativity.

More simply, book reading experiences can be turned into discussions, into comparisons of personal experiences. The awakening realization of self can be a lonely time for a child. Do I look all right? Am I liked? If I hit another child, how will he/she feel about me? The opportunity to identify with characters in a book and the resulting awareness of common experiences among peers is of great comfort and support during childhood development. A small group of children rereading a favorite story, for example, or a lone child thumbing through a book, should be encouraged to talk about favorite characters or things they like. These purposeful oral discussions encouraged by the teacher will not only assist the children in developing a love for literature, but will help them express emotion and build a new vocabulary. As important as emotion, learning how to express experiences will help them become aware of thoughts they might not have been able to conceptualize by themselves.

It is necessary, however, to interject a note of caution. A wise teacher of young children will periodically question these new, awakening concepts. Akin to *Amelia Bedelia*, youngsters frequently interpret words and phrases at their most literal level. Children from third through intermediate grades will see the humor in the *Amelia Bedelia* books; Gwynne's *The King who Rained* and *Chocolate Moose for Dinner*, Baer's *Words Are Like Faces*, or Kohn's *What a Funny Thing to Say*, while preschoolers and primary aged students may actually believe the concept as stated. The difference between fantasy and reality must be introduced early, and is one of the most important and, sometimes, difficult tasks to be mastered.

Children's literature presents another dimension over and above those previously discussed. Besides the colored illustrations, behind the new words is another benefit to learning: Reducing fear and uncertainty. Most fears, after all, stem from "not knowing." Childhood stories can be the medium for turning sometimes fearful shadows into recognizable and familiar shapes. Fear of the dark can be alleviated by changing its meaning in the minds of the children and by showing them they can master it. Bradbury's vintage book, *Switch on the Night*, never loses its appeal and assurance by likening the night to a light switch.

Fear of starting school is addressed in numerous books which take the child step-by-step into this unknown adventure. Burningham's *The Blanket* reassures the young reader that many children need a favorite possession, while fears of desertion are addressed in Zolotow's *If You Listen* and Preston's *Where Did My Mother Go?*

Children's literature contains another gift for the growing psyche: The concept, "I am somebody; I can do things, TOO." In addition to needing love and reassurance, children also want to do things for those they love. They want the best brought out in themselves. They want to turn their limitations into victories. Mercer Mayer and Elizabeth Winthrop answer just such needs in their portrayal of children's abilities and limitations in *Just for You* and *Are You Sad, Mama?* Karla Kuskin's *Herbert Hated Being Small* and Jean Berg's *Big Bug, Little Bug*, deal with a child's problems about size and acceptance. *The Tale of Tawny and Dingo* and *A Bargain for Frances* by William Armstrong and Russell Hoban characterize strong friendship and ability to overcome insurmountable odds.

Most of the books discussed so far have been books containing print. Picture books which contain few or no words provide, perhaps, the best spark for children's individual creativity. Children stretch their imaginations, reach for the right word in their growing vocabularies, and interact verbally with the group. Most of Leo Lionni's books are of the easy picture-story book format and are loved by young children. A special favorite—dealing with color concepts, understanding, and friendship—is *little blue and little yellow*, a motivational film produced by McGraw-Hill. *Rosie's Walk* and *Just Like Everyone Else* have few words, but many repetitive actions throughout. These allow children to master concepts while elaborating on the storyline in an easy, relaxed manner. Pat Ross' *Hi Fly* contains only four words and black and white ink drawings. Children can create delightful stories from the pictures and will even "read" the words at a very young age. Each successful achievement encourages and motivates children to strive toward others.

Wordless picture books allow for complete freedom, not only enabling children to create stories, but also to develop their vocabularies. Recommended titles are: *Apples; Changes, Changes; A Boy, A Dog, and A Frog; Frog Goes to Dinner; Making Friends; April Fools; The Ballooning Adventures of Paddy Pork*; and *The Chicken's Child*. Two books deserve special discussion: Winter's *The Bear and the Fly* and Turkle's *Deep in the Forest*. Father Bear's compulson to get rid of a fly which is disturbing the family's dinner (*The Bear and the Fly*) causes him to demolish the family table and room—from which the fly departs unscathed. Turkle's book turns the story of *The Three Bears* around, and it doesn't take young children long to figure out this twist. Both of these books evoke great and hilarious responses, and preschoolers read these picture books by themselves. Art work in children's books such as these ranges from simple line drawings to bright multicolored pictures, both of which delight the eye and add to the joy of reading.

Pictures and words. Colors and concepts. First steps on what can be a never-ending road to the joy of learning. Teachers at preschool and primary grade levels help the children they teach take their first steps along that road. Like Sleeping Beauty, who was asleep until awakened by love's first kiss, the children awake to words and give back to their teachers a gift equally as valuable as the one given to them. Eyes that were closed, now open wide with growing understanding.

References

Armstrong, W.H. *The tale of Tawny and Dingo*. New York: Harper & Row, 1979.
Baer, E. *Words are like faces*. New York: Pantheon, 1980.
Berg, J.H. *Big bug, little bug*. New York: Follett, 1964.
Bradbury, R. *Switch on the night*. New York: Pantheon, 1955.
Burningham, J. *The blanket*. New York: Crowell, 1976.
Goodell, J. *The ballooning adventures of Paddy Pork*. New York: Harcourt Brace Jovanovich, 1969.
Gwynne, F. *The chocolate moose for dinner*. New York: Windmill, 1976.
Gwynne, F. *The king who rained*. New York: Windmill, 1970.
Hartelius, M. *The chicken's child*. New York: Doubleday, 1975.
Hoban, R., & Hoban, L. *A bargain for Frances*. New York: Harper & Row, 1970
Hogrogian, N. *Apples*. New York: Macmillan, 1972.
Hutchins, P. *Changes, changes*. New York: Macmillan, 1971.
Hutchins, P. *Rosie's walk*. New York: Young Reader's Press, 1968.
Knaub, L. (illustrated by D. Freeman). *A day is waiting*. New York: Viking, 1980.
Kohn, B. *What a funny thing to say*. New York: Dial, 1974.
Krahn, F. *April fools*. New York: Dutton, 1974.
Kuskin, K. *Herbert hated being small*. New York: Houghton Mifflin, 1979.
Kuskin, K. *Just like everyone else*. New York: Harper & Row, 1959.
Lionni, L. *Little blue and litte yellow*. Boston: Astor, 1959.
Mayer, M. *A boy, a dog, and a frog*. New York: Dial, 1967.
Mayer, M. *Frog goes to dinner*. New York: Dial, 1974.

Mayer, M. *Just for You*. Racine, Wisconsin: Western, 1975.
Parish, P. *Amelia Bedelia*. New York: Harper & Row, 1963.
Preston, E.M. *Where did my mother go?* New York: Four Winds, 1978.
Ross, P. *Hi fly*. New York: Crown, 1974.
Schick, E. *Making friends*. New York: Macmillan, 1969.
Turkle, B. *Deep in the forest*. New York: Dutton, 1976.
Winter, P. *The bear and the fly*. New York: Crown, 1976.
Winthrop, E. *Are you sad, mama?* New York: Harper & Row, 1979.
Zolotow, C. *If you listen*. New York: Harper & Row, 1980.

Chant

Poetry:
The Child's Way to the Real World

Kay March
Paramus, New Jersey, Public Schools

One of the major objectives in any language arts curriculum is the development of creative reading and writing skills. One way to teach to this objective is to give children an insight into the beauty and power of our language. Teachers must constantly be impressed by the appreciation children have of our language and inspired by the values they express in their poetic writings.

Children are all potential poets and have within them an enchanting quality that is as natural as growing. They are full of fresh curiosity about everything that is relevant in their fascinating world. They question and explore. They receive and enjoy the rhythm of Mother Goose and nursery rhymes. They grow through plan-provoking counting rhymes. They thrive on thoughts expressed in riddles. In brief, children's joy and delight with the world can easily be discerned through their natural poetic instincts and uninhibited thoughts.

It is truly refreshing to follow the way a child sees. With expert guidance from a teaching staff that selects and reads poetry, children grow. Their imaginations flourish. Their job for living expands. They bring to our world a sense of magic!

Children Like Poetry

Why do children like poetry? Let me see if I can count the ways:
They like it for the thoughts they can have that are their own.
They like if for the rhythm that is music to their ears.

They like it for the joys that their eyes alone can see.
They like it for the world of magic they can explore.

Children like to listen to poetry read by a teacher who feels and who can bring to life the words that seem to be dormant on a printed page. One nine year old boy reacted to poetry read aloud by writing these lines:

> I like poetry.
> Some poetry rhymes;
> Some poetry doesn't.
> Some poetry has five lines.
> Some poetry has a beat.
> Some poetry has four lines;
> Some has only three.
> I like any kind of poetry.

> —Mike O'Hara, 1973

Poetry can be the key to learning to read easily and with great enjoyment.

A kindergarten teacher may start with a topic all children seem to know a great deal about—colors. A group of "ready-to-learn-to-read" youngsters may have a delightful discussion led by the teacher on colors and how colors make one feel. Preliminary to the discussion, Mary O'Neill's book, *Hailstones and Halibut Bones*, should be read aloud. From that point, a particular color concept could be developed. Let's try the color *red*.

"What is red?" the teacher asks. "Let's put the word on our chart."

RED

"Who can read the color word I just wrote?"

The children may respond in many different ways. The teacher may choose to point out the letters that make up the word and then ask again, "What is red?"

"Red is an apple," says one lover of fruit.

We are on our way.

I have known of many instances in which a poem made up by a group or an individual became the catalyst for the road to reading.

> 1. Red is an *apple*.
>   Big and round.
> 2. Red is the *nose*
>   Of Rudolph the reindeer.

3. Red is a *cherry*
   On top of a cake.
4. Red is a *color*
   That brightens the world.

Now, let's read this together.

After a second reading, each two lines can be read, and then the red items can be circled for instant recognition.

A sight vocabulary based on a poetic experience written by the eventual readers is a sure winner. Let us not belabor this point, but move to the intermediate grades where "lack of comprehension" seems to be the cry of the teacher. How about teaching this skill through poetry written by students in the classroom?

Let me offer a few poems written by students and published in *Young Poets of Paramus* which could be used to develop duplication, implication, and application—the three levels of comprehension.

SILVERY SNOWFLAKES

Silvery snowflakes in the sky,
  Sparkling diamonds drifting by.
Rubies, emeralds twinkling bright,
  Twirling stars in the daylight.
Frozen teardrops, what a sight!
  Fluffy blanket covers the night.

—Michael Alesso, Grade 5

Questions: *Three Types*

1. *Duplication*
   How many pictures does this young poet paint for you?
   Sparkling diamonds
   Twinkling rubies/emeralds
   Twirling stars
   Frozen teardrops
   Fluffy blanket
2. *Implication*
   How would a "sparkling diamond" drift by?
   Would the diamond snowflake look like a real diamond?
   Would twirling stars in the daylight look like stars at night?

If you are going to do "implication" questioning, do not assume that all youngsters know what diamonds, rubies, and emeralds are.

Bring in some gems and have children see and feel, and the implications will vary with each individual.

> Are snowflakes silver?
> Why can the answer be yes, no, or sometimes?

Students react to the above questions with unabashed joy because they can respond from their experiences in living. This is thinking.

3. *Application*
   Have you seen a silver snowflake?
   Have you seen diamonds sparkle?
   Have you seen rubies and emeralds twinkle?
   Why can teardrops freeze?
   Have you ever seen a frozen teardrop?
   Have you ever seen a fluffy blanket that covered the night?

Student poems lend themselves to the development of all comprehension skills. In 1978 two contributors to "Young Poets of Paramus" wrote on the theme of loneliness. This is a recurrent theme to which both students and teachers can relate. The skills of *comparing* and *contrasting* can be more easily taught through these two poems than through the words in the texts written by "other people."

LONELINESS

Loneliness is a dark cloud surrounding you.
It closes upon you
And clutches at you,
And separates you from others.

It is when someone dies
Or moves away
Leaving a gap
That can never be filled.

Loneliness is when all those who love you
Turn away
Leaving you alone
In space.

—Donna Gitter, Grade 5

LONELINESS

I sit on the sidewalk
Lonely as can be.
There's nothing in the world to do,

Nothing new to see.
I'm waiting...
Waiting for someone
To come and play

        with me.
        —Shirley Holmon, Grade 5

Questions: Three Types

1. *Duplication*
   How many pictures of loneliness does Donna give?
   How many does Shirley give us?
2. *Implication*
   Why does Donna refer to loneliness as a "dark cloud"?
   Why does Shirley equate loneliness with "nothing to do"?
3. *Application*
   Do *you* feel that loneliness is being alone?
   Do *you* have to be with people not to be lonely?
   Are *you* lonely at night or during the day?
   Do all of us have periods of loneliness?

Students poems can motivate and titillate. There is no surer way of getting true involvement than dealing with the interest of young people. I would offer you student poems about a variety of sports.

SKATEBOARDING

The wind in my hair
The excitement in my bones.
The vibration in my feet
The relaxation in my mind.
My own little world,
Where I am king
Of every new road
I am conquering.

        —Michael Stiles, Grade 5

Poetry and Children

Have *you* ever been king of the road?
The author of "Skateboarding" conquers "every new road"
 through this sport. How do *you* conquer a new road?
Do you have to feel the "wind in your hair" to conquer a road?

BASEBALL

It isn't fair for a little tyke
 To miss the series every night.
Excitement in the air it's bringing
 Starting the very first inning.

The Yanks took three and the Dodgers two.
 I'm stuck tonight because of you.
I hope they do not score a run
 Until this homework, it is done.

I also hope the game goes quick,
 And how I hope the Yanks do fine.
Extra innings would destroy the night,
 Because it runs into my bedtime.

But like all good things it will end,
 And I hope that you don't have a fit.
This poem must end.
 We got a hit.

—Brian Niland, Grade 6

Questions

Has your homework ever interfered with your sports interests or
 activities?
Do all good things come to an end?

BOWLING

Bowling, bowling, lots of fun—
Lots of fun for everyone.
Try to knock down at least one pin,
If you knock them all you just might win.
If you get nine then go for the other,
But if you're unlucky the ball might go
 in the gutter.

You might get a strike, and you might
    get a spare—
But all that really counts is that
    you play fair!

—David Snider, Grade 6

Questions

    Is bowling fun for everyone?
    What is a "gutter" in bowling?
    Why is playing fair the thing that counts in sports?

The questions generated by student poems can be endless, but there is no value to them unless the teacher gives students many opportunities to express their reactions. Increased student participation is a must. Teacher sensitivity to beauty of language and to children is an absolute prerequisite in teaching through poetry.

On Reading Story

Leland B. Jacobs, Emeritus
Teachers College, Columbia University

There is a need to be more discriminating in the discussion of literature, whether that literature is found in basal readers, anthologies, magazines, or hardcover or paperback full-length books.

It would seem that those developing children's textbooks in which stories are found too often have been more concerned about decoding skills or other matters than they have about comprehension of literature. So their proposals of questions about story content and of discussion practices have been counterproductive so far as comprehension, appreciation, and enjoyment of literature are concerned. If such exploitation of literary reading is to be stopped, we as teachers need to do some rethinking of our concept of story and of appropriate practices to use in teaching the reading of story.

What is story? Stripped to the barest essentials, I define story as characters *coping in terms of a quest*. Full consideration of what is involved in story requires more elaboration, more explication than is possible here. I must be content to propose that:

- Story finds its bearing in a character or characters made sufficiently interesting that the reader wants to find out what happens to the individual(s). Without a well-developed character, a story remains superficial and of little consequence no matter how much effort has been put into making it adventurous, humorous, or mysterious.
- The central character's copings become the plot. In other words, what makes the plot believable is the character's attempts to cope with aspects of living, sometimes physical,

From L.B. Jacobs. On reading story. *Reading Instruction Journal*, 1980, *23*. Reprinted by permission.

but also sometimes emotional, social, or intellectual. Story happenings, incidents, events, interactions, and dialogue come into clear focus because they are necessary for the character to live through if he/she is to get on with whatever she/he is attempting to do, to be, or to accomplish.

- What helps the reader to comprehend fully the character's copings is the kind of quest the character is engaged in. It might be a physical quest such as a journey or the overcoming of a handicap. It might be an emotional quest such as facing up to death, or overcoming the consequences of being a foster child. As a social quest, it might be dealing with an interracial friendship or participating in an ecological project. As a spiritual quest, it could be the matter of wrestling with a conflict in values. Whatever comes through to the reader as the major thrust of the main character's seeking behavior gives the story its sense of quest, which markedly affects the inclusion of events, the sequencing of events, and the sequencing of plot.

- Character(s) coping in terms of a quest can be cast as fanciful, romantic, or realistic. If fanciful, it is definitely "make-believe." If romantic, the story is improbable but not impossible. If realistic, the story is entirely possible. Notice that the same quest can be treated in any one of these ways. But the characters' behaviors and their copings as they attempt to achieve desired ends will differ markedly in terms of which way is being used for the story.

If such is what is involved in story, then what is done to guide children's comprehension must square with that conception. And it would seem that, for discussion, the teacher would want to begin with thinking about character, using questions like:

What seems to be important for us to know about this character? How does where the character lives affect him/her? When he/she lives? In what ways does the character change because of what happens to him/her?

It would seem that next the teacher would want to lead discussion to the kind of quest involved:

What does the character (use the character's name, such as Michael, Dora, Mrs. Blake, the old man, Paddy Porcupine) want to do? To be? To accomplish? Why is this accomplishment important to the character? Is this a quest that seems reasonable in terms of what we know about the character? Is the outcome of the quest what was anticipated?

Having established the children's comprehension of what seems significant about characters and quest, the teacher can turn to the copings to see how the plot helps or hinders, leads forward or backward, moves rapidly or slowly toward the character's accomplishment of what is sought. For discussion of plot, questions like the following seem appropriate:

What helped the character toward achievement of what is wanted? What hindered? Who helped the main character? How so? Who didn't help? When did the main character seem to be surest of success? When closest to failure? Was the outcome of the quest satisfying to the main character? How so?

As has been said before, in all such questions, characters' names will be used by the teacher so that the reality of the events, the story's believability, is kept intact. For what one wants as the larger outcome of story comprehension is the development of what has been called "the educated imagination," by one literary theoretician, and what one eminent present-day writer has called "not what *is* but what *might be*." We want children to learn early that literature creates a world of the mind—a world that *is* but never *was* actually.

From what has been said thus far, one will notice that certain types of questions commonly found in basal readers, textbooks that use stories, are not being suggested for use in aids to story comprehension.

Factual or informational questions, as:
What did you learn about Alaska from this story?
Questions that encourage moralizing, as:
What does the story teach us about telling lies?
Questions that take the reader outside the story, as:
Would you do what Eric did?
Mere plot questions, as:
What next? What next? What last?
Innocuous questions, as:
Did you like it? Was that a funny story?

Such questions do nothing to help children comprehend the story, since all these types of queries take readers outside, or away from the story rather than keep them inside, and it is only inside its created world that the story lives; becomes believable; that it helps to develop an educated imagination.

Of course, we who teach need to help children comprehend factual and informational material. But how fortunate is the child who has a teacher who makes clear the differences as well as the likenesses in comprehending the factual and the fictional, who zeros in on the kinds of discussion questions that foster appropriate understanding of fact and of story.

To learn to read story well—to know what story is, to appreciate the well-developed story, to enjoy being extended in one's imagination by a capable writer—is surely a worthy outcome of one's schooling in reading. What literary reading comprehension does for a person is very much what James Russell Lowell said it would do: "Enable us to see with the keenest of eyes, hear with the finest ears, and listen to the sweetest voices of all times."

The Reading Act Within

M. Jerry Weiss
Jersey City State College

Alvin Toffler, in his book, *The Third Wave*, says:

> Finally there are movements aimed at literally turning back the clock—like the back-to-basics movement in United States schools. Legitimately outraged by the disaster in mass education, it does not recognize that a de-massified society calls for new educational strategies, but seeks instead to restore and enforce Second Wave uniformity in the schools. Nevertheless, all these attempts to achieve uniformity are essentially the rearguard actions of a spent civilization. The thrust of Third Wave change is toward increased diversity, not toward the further standardization of life. And this is just as true of ideas, political convictions, sexual proclivities, educational methods, eating habits, religious views, ethnic attitudes, musical tastes, fashions, and family forms as it is of automated production.
>
> An historic turning point has been reached, and standardization, another of the ruling principles of Second Wave civilization, is being replaced. (pp. 273-274)

What could be "academically" more personal or more intimate than the reading act? An individual visualizes or internalizes the variety of ideas stimulated by a writer's select choice of words to convey ideas. The action or lack of action, the emotional responses or lack of such responses, are all due to the way a reader responds to a particular writer's production. Who could or should predict the responses to literature? What could be more dangerous to a dynamic, creative society than the standardization of responses?

Try this brief activity. Copy the following list of words on a sheet of paper:

money	success
love	peace
health	friendship
family	honesty

From M.J. Weiss. The reading act within. *Reading Instruction Journal*, 1980, *23*. Reprinted by permission.

As you examine these words, rank them in order of importance to you. Beside the most important, place the number one (1); beside the least important, place the number eight (8). Each word is to have only a single designated number, between one and eight, assigned to it.

Now write a brief paragraph explaining why you ranked the words in this order. Ask a friend to do the same. Compare your responses to your friend's. If there are differences in the ranking, to what would you attribute these?

This is, indeed, one of the *humanistic* elements, a sense of personal values, a reaction to a variety of situations, which is a key part of the reading process. Words out of context cause readers to project meanings and experiences; it is no easy assignment to explain what these words conjure up in the minds of readers or why such idea associations take place. This, a part of critical, interpretive thinking, is germane to effective, enjoyable, and efficient reading.

Words in context often force readers to recall specific moments in their lives which are similar to what is being read. When my mother died, I was pained by the loss, and cancer was a "horror" word since it brought so much pain and a sense of helplessness. I turned to reading in an attempt to escape my real world and to find other thoughts, characters, events, actions as a source for temporary distraction! I chose to read a number of best sellers—mysteries, love stories, tales of adventure—and I was amazed at the number of times *death, pain, suffering*, and *CANCER*, appeared in these books. My immediate reaction was to put such books aside; but, then, I reasoned that this would accomplish little. It was I who was projecting personal feelings, experiences, a deep sense of grief into these words and incidents, even if the characters involved didn't deserve such feelings on my part. How was I going to stop myself from doing this? Did I really want to stop? Should I stop?

If these questions seem perplexing, if they seem abnormal in the study of reading, then I am that drummer who marches to a very different tune. The *core* of reading seems to be so seldom discussed in professional texts, committed, as they often should be, to methodology rather than the unpredictable effects of words and ideas upon readers. I am among a rare group who is equally concerned with the impact of reading upon the reader.

The humanist in the reading process "feels" the writer. Ask yeshiva students to explain what is happening to them as they read Milton Meltzer's powerful, nonfiction work, *Never to Forget: The Jews of the Holocaust*. Why the yeshiva students? Their home, cultural, and religious activities often have included emotional discussions about anti-semitism and this period of history which many gentile families sometimes miss, overlook, or talk about in less passionate terms. Ask black students to react to poems by Nikki Giovanni or Maya Angelou, which center on segregation, indignities, caustic remarks, and behaviors which sparked civil rights activities.

History students could be intellectually stimulated by William Manchester's *The Glory and the Dream.* How many recall the details Manchester provides in this tome filled with conflicts, controversy, and conscious-raising events? Who emerge as heroes? What events and/or actions might identify heroes for today or tomorrow? Do popular cultures and mass media consciously determine the making of such heroes?

Ask any science student which great scientist he or she would like to meet. Popular books on Galileo, Pasteur, Einstein, Freud, Madame Curie, Jonas Salk, among others, would provide sources for "personal" talk shows with some of the greatest minds whose ideas shook treasured tenets and changed the developments of civilizations.

One discovery, one humble idea, examined thoroughly, tried out, discussed and debated, resolved, could project an individual from anonymity to immortality. What discoveries during the remainder of this century can significantly alter the fields of health, medicine, industry and technology.

One personal experience can become the focus for creative expression. Hear the cry, "I am alive! I am!" Bob Fosse, famed dancer, Broadway director, and choreographer, used film to depict his close encounter with death. Critics and movie-goers may vary in their appraisals of this movie, *All That Jazz,* but Fosse chose lights, camera, action to share his words and feelings about life and death.

There is a literary process in any artistic work as the creators organize their thoughts to communicate their talents. Readers, viewers, or prospective customers continue to have the right to make judgments, but in a standardized society, how many choices will there be? How many creators will come forth? What penalties and rewards do creative people receive for their efforts in defense of self-expression?

There is a world, a real world, not restricted by academic rules and regulations. For some, the letter "A" is not the first letter learned. For others, filling in blanks to get a "more perfect whole" will produce panic, frustration, and subsequent degradation. Yet, some of these same people have other ways, other built-in mechanisms for developing their perceptions, "more perfect wholes." Sights and sounds can trigger myriad responses to the essential questions conceived with the qualities of life. *The American Way of Laughing: From Benjamin Franklin to Woody Allen* and *More Tales Out of School: Humor in the Classroom* could appeal to those who enjoy social commentary and criticism with a bit of wit. Fables, folklore, and foibles are products of human endeavors. What printer could be blamed for producing the delicious effect as a result of these specific words: "Cyrus McCormick invented the raper!" What a difference an "e" can make! One little error and there can be laughter. But there also can be condemnation, cursing, dismissals, tears, in a world that goes on. The ultimate payment to the printer might be the loss of a job; however, the reader who stumbles on the error will do double takes, not quite believing that one's knowledge of inventors and inventions could be so incredibly challenged and amusing.

The serious readers, the book borrowers, buyers, stealers, are completely fascinated with the miracles of words and language. Word choices and arrangements strike cerebral/cardiac chords, echoing throughout the entire organism, and produce love/hate, passionate/dispassionate responses.

Look at any picture in a magazine or newspaper advertisement. Use words to convey the exact scene before your eyes, the desired effect, and the actual effect. How many words did you use to describe the actual picture? How exact are your words? If you gave these words to a photographer or an artist, would such a person be capable of reproducing the picture you are describing? If there should be discrepancies, to what would you attribute these?

Language is the master of deception through conception. The poetry of Stephen Crane, Judith Viorst, Robert Frost, and Edgar Allan Poe offers many different visions for readers. How concise, precise a poem must be. So few words, yet how a mind spins from the ideas and images presented. Who can ever forget the amazing cast of characters in Edgar Lee Masters' *Spoon River Anthology*? He has created so many familiar voices, so many secrets, problems, comic/tragic personalities who arouse compassion because readers care and now understand the frailty of being human. Nancy Larrick has edited a marvelous collection of "people poems" in *Crazy to Be Alive in Such a Strange World*. Each poem, some matched with photographs, evokes a person or people worth reading about, getting to know, thinking about, relating to. Who among these people would make an interesting friend?

Lyrics, as parts of songs, continue the appreciation of poetry. Stevie Wonder's "You Are the Sunshine of My Life" and Hal David's "What the World Needs Now Is Love Sweet Love" offer excellent opportunities for teaching a love of language. (So many times I've heard teachers say, "These children can't remember anything!" How wrong they are! So many students know most of the words to songs at the top of the charts. Using their knowledge and their interests, a good teacher could use lyrics to teach a number of reading skills.)

First graders were taught the lyrics to "You Are the Sunshine of My Life." The teacher gave students sheets of white shelving paper, and assigned students lines from the song and asked them to illustrate what they thought the lines meant. The drawings were phenomenal. She taped together the drawings, printed the words beneath the appropriate illustrations, and created a picture-song reader. The children loved it! They learned each word, including sight words, and were eager to make more song books. Other favorites were "Up, Up, and Away," "Tea for Two," "Raindrops Keep Falling on My Head," "I Write the Songs," and "Rudolph, the Red Nosed Reindeer."

Upper grade students were asked to teach classmates their favorite songs. Students took dittoed copies of the songs and were asked to find photographs, pictures in newspapers or magazines, or ones taken by themselves to produce "photo-lyrics." What wonderful imaginations emerged from the lyrics to "Over the Rainbow," "Copacabana," "Evergreen," "The Way We Were," and popular songs by Kiss, the Bee Gees, Styx, Roberta Flack, George Benson, and Donnie and Marie Osmond.

Role playing is a wonderful introduction to drama. Students are given a problem, and then they are asked to "act out" the situation and subsequent events. Shortly thereafter, students can be introduced to one-act plays, to be followed later by full length plays including musical comedies. Readers Theatre is fun and offers the opportunity to create dramatic activities from a wide range of printed resources. Students' interpretations of various roles offer many opportunities for discussion and for enhancing critical thinking and interpretative reading.

Humanism in reading recognizes that readers become involved. Something happens inside. Teachers should provide a variety of activities through which a student demonstrates what's happening as a result of the interaction with the printed page. When teachers hear students explain the sources for their ideas, they remove the too heavy emphasis on right-wrong answers. It's time we spent more effort on studying how children think, how children react. Through greater concentration on such assignments, will personal literacy be achieved? The individual is the reader. He/she takes in the printed symbols and may produce a variety of responses, possibly demonstrating unique abilities and talents, providing a key function by recognizing that reading leads to active endeavors. Students build on what they know, what they want to know, and in an environment that emphasizes the positive and appreciative characteristics of reading. The humanist teacher thoroughly enjoys the minds of students and the variety of ideas any classroom can produce. Thirty answers, all different? What now? Even the *Book of Lists* can demonstrate the delight of what people do, did, believe, believed, achieve, achieved.

Given the word *Key*, how many associations can you make with this printed symbol? The more the merrier. Play with your ideas. Create situations in which this three letter item can demonstrate meanings and applications for you.

This is the power of language. The mind constructs through the slightest suggestion. A "key to life," a "lock and key," "the exact key for your voice," or the "key to your heart" are all intellectual, feeling symbols which say so much for and about you. Creation—ah, the enjoyment in that process—is an ultimate result for any person who succeeds and finds delight in language. So handle "the answer keys" with care. For beyond the response is a reasoning process. Gaining an understanding of that amazing mental ability should be a humbling and humanizing process. When the teacher knows enough to understand, and when through such understanding he/she demonstrates care and appreciation, literates will arrive in greater abundance and with greater insights to make "The Third Wave" a remarkable phase of civilization.